Do you know I Love You?

A LIFE OF BEING NOT DOING

NICHOLE HAMBLIN

Ark House Press
PO Box 1722, Port Orchard, WA 98366 USA
PO Box 1321, Mona Vale NSW 1660 Australia
PO Box 318 334, West Harbour, Auckland 0661 New Zealand
arkhousepress.com

Unless otherwise indicated, all Scripture quotations are taken from the Life Application Study Bible, New International Version, copyright 1988, 1989, 1990, 1991 by Tyndale House Publishers, Inc.

Scripture quotations marked The Message are taken from The Message. Copyright by Eugene Peterson 1993, 1994, 1995, 1996,2000,2001,2002 by Tyndale House Publishers, Inc.

Scripture quotations marked New Living Translation are taken from Holy Bible, New Living Translation, copyright © 1996, 2004, 2007, 2013, 2015 by Tyndale House Foundation.

Scripture quotations marked Living Bible are taken from The Living Bible copyright © 1971 by Tyndale House Foundation.

Scripture quotations marked New Life Version are taken from New Life Version copyright © 1969 by Christian Literature International.

Scripture quotations marked New American Standard Bible are taken from New American Standard Bible copyright © 1960, 1962, 1963, 1968, 1971, 1972, 1973, 1975, 1977, 1995 by The Lockman Foundation.

Cataloguing in Publication Data:
Title: Do You Know I Love You?
ISBN: 9780648263999 (pbk.)
Subjects: Christian Living, Devotion
Other Authors/Contributors: Hamblin, Nichole

Layout by initiateagency.com

If there's a book you really want to read, but it hasn't been written yet, then you must write it.[1] ~Toni Morrison

Contents

Acknowledgments

I am truly thankful for all the people in my life. For it has taken every one to shape me into the girl that I am.

For all the people who have invested into my life, thank you.

For the people who knew I could do better than 'that' thank you for believing in me when I didn't have that belief.

For the people who knew I was just wearing a mask, thank you for seeing behind it.

For the people who loved the roughness off me, thank you for unconditional love.

For the people who were willing to listen to the opinions, thank you for your prayers for my heart to change.

For the people who directed my eyes to my true meaning and purpose, thanks for the firm head movement.

For the people who let me practice Jesus' love on them, for practice makes better.

For the people who were genuine, honest, bold and true with me, for you have pushed me right into the arms of all things genuine. I thank you for this.

For the people who showed me innocence and childlike faith, thank you for reminding me that life is so much simpler.

For the people who are different than me, thank you for shining bright a beautiful quality placed there by your Creator, for you draw me to Him in praise.

To the Team at Ark House

James Newman, thank you for your patience to answer every single one of my questions. I am grateful to you for guiding me on this journey. Nicole Danswan and team, thank you for the gorgeous cover design. I am also grateful for the attention to detail as you cleaned up my mess and formatted things so nicely. Lynn Goldsmith, thank you really doesn't encompass what I need to say to you. For you endured every word and played clean-up and I really appreciate you.

To the T-Squad

Thank you for the amazing privilege of being your momma. You two have taught me what pure unconditional love and grace looks like. For each day you have administered grace and love to me.
For I have forgotten lunches and P.E. shoes. I have misplaced library books, I have burnt the toast, and I have gotten angry and yelled.
Thank you for doing life with me.
Thank you for allowing God to use you both to teach me that I was created to be a momma, and not just a momma, but your momma.
May you both know I love you and you have my heart.

To My best friend

Engineer, thank you for laughing at my personal idioms, for not giving up when things get hard, and for building the pillow wall. Your humor, your smile and your 'leaving things better than you find them' - all of this has me in love with you.

To My Savior and Lord

Jesus, You are what got this all started, thank You. May my heart, mind and soul continue to be madly in love with You.

Prologue

Have you ever come across something in the written form, you read it, and it resonates within you as if it was meant for you? The words, each letter, each one was meant for you and maybe even you alone. In the moment of reading them, all else is silenced and you are alone with these words. It is in those moments that you begin to hear these words and not only is your mind registering them, but your heart joins in too.

A moment in the spring of 2010 I found my nose in a book[1] and there were these words; *Sit, Stand, Walk, Run.* They were listed in this order on purpose. One was supposed to achieve, learn, and obtain the meaning of each word in this order. Within moments my brain and heart knew something wasn't in order for me. Life felt unbalanced. My heart ached for something. And yet I wasn't quite sure what the something was.

Sit and Run - these are the words that caught my attention. As if the words were book ends holding everything together. Or maybe those two words represented a spectrum and I found myself on one distant end of this spectrum, and my heart ached for balance. It was the last word of the four that caught my attention first. I found myself stuck on this three-letter word. *Run.* It was a pace in which I knew. It was a word that mentioned to keep moving, it was noise and people oriented, at least to me. Within the moments that my eyes were fixed on this word, I quickly realized I had been 'running' for many years. You see I am a runner. And running comes easy for me. I run passionately, sometimes so passionately I am up ahead of God. And for some reason I was not aware of, I internally knew I didn't know how to sit. Something needed to change in my life. I was being asked to sit. I had to learn how to sit to get my priorities in order. I needed this time to get balanced.

I fought God on this. I whined and complained. *"Why do I have to sit, while everyone else around me gets to run?"* I argued and stubbornly kept running. I defended my running. I was still running for God. All the things I was 'doing' were for Him. Justified running.

And yet my running was not what He wanted.

There will be times in our lives when He pulls us aside so we can listen.

He pulled me aside all right… I was at a Speaker's Conference over 2000 miles from my comfortable home and surroundings. I found it kind of humiliating and mocking. Why am I here then if all I am going home to do is sit?

God knew what it would take for me to be still enough, quiet enough and maybe even to be ready enough to hear more about this whole sitting season.

Why was I fighting this whole sitting thing?

I pictured this sitting as more of a punishment. It was a timeout. It was away from people, away from the action, it was too quiet and it would be lonely.

On Saturday July 31st 2010 I heard;

"Nichole I am here with you. I will be with you during this sitting season. I have reserved this time for you. It's going to be you and Me together. I have some things I want to tell you, to teach you, and you have some healing to do. I will be with you every minute. This is all good, I promise."

I was standing in the hall of a very beautiful hotel in North Carolina, tears running down my face, cute little red shoes on my feet and my head hears these words, but my heart doesn't.

You deserve a fair warning, mainly because your time is valuable. This is the first of its kind, a book written by a girl who never ever wanted to write a book. What?! Maybe you're thinking right now you wished you saved the receipt. Or maybe you were given a free copy and you are thinking… *"thank goodness."*

Where does one officially start writing a book, especially a book they don't want to write? Introduction? I included one as if to make this the real thing. Who knows? This might just be a one of a kind thing. I am sure it is.

Why me? Why a girl from a little town who has many other talents like shoe buying, reading, running, baking a yummy chocolate cake? Writing is not included in my repertoire (look at me throwing in the big words, just so you know I am not a girl of big words, I had to look up the spelling of that one), of things I consider myself good at.

Of all people on the face of this earth to write a book I truly am thinking, "I am not it." Writing a book requires patience, obedience and letting go of fears (fears that are tightly attached to pride, per-fectionism, the need for control and caring what others think (peo-ple pleasing) can you have parenthesis inside of parentheses?) See my point? I am not the one to write a book. So what has me here at my laptop long enough to focus and sit still to write this book?

I have to believe that God knew what He was getting Himself into when He created me. A personality that would question the purpose and motive that would doubt my abilities for the job and would worry what others would think about the whole process. Why would He ask me to write a book? How could He ask someone who would rather be out running? He has some great writers out there, ones who truly knew how to set up a sentence. I certainly struggle with this.

Where did this lofty thing come from you may be asking?

My heart begs you, "Can you put your grammar knowledge aside for a few pages and read? Will you be brave and courageous and just see if any point of this finds its way into your heart?"

Included within the pages of this book is a truthful account of a girl's (that girlie being me, I think they call that third person) journey to learn to sit and hear from her Creator. A girl learning she is loved, via a process she would have never foreseen or chosen. It is my hope that by the end of these pages you hear something maybe you have never heard before too. Will you go on this journey with me? Will you find out what got me to sit long enough to write a book?

PART 1:

Sit

Sit Down

I thought I would give you a few pages to show you what eventually got me to the point of sitting down. I mentioned in the Introduction the moment in which I saw in writing the word '*sit*' and how I just knew something was about to be really different for me. Taking my 5'4" self-down a few notches to a position in which running would not be possible. The quiet mentioning of sitting had been going on for a couple of months, most likely years, but my ears were not tuned in. However, one day it got so loud I could hear it above the engines of a 747.

I was 2000 miles from my home on an airplane thousands of feet (speaking of feet, just so you know airport security does *not* count how many pairs of shoes you pack) in the air - stuck and belted in my seat for 'safety'. I had nowhere to go. I was trapped.

Every emotion that comes along with being trapped was surging through my mind. Internally I was arguing with my Creator. I yelled out, "Why in the world did you take me to a speaker's conference over 2000 miles from my home just to tell me You want me to sit?"

His response was, "I will do what it takes to get your attention."

It was the same message He had been speaking to me for a few months now. In all reality it was probably years, but it had just been the past few months that I was starting to pay attention.

As I walked off that airplane I was entering a new season in my life.

I was about to 'sit'. I was not happy about it at all.

Sitting meant I would resign my position as Women's Ministry Director at church. I would stop teaching Bible studies, and I would not be accepting invites to speak. I was to limit my volunteering and stop saying *yes* to everyone who asked. I was to come home and sit down and focus on my family.

To sit and be "inactive" and not get to participate seemed like a punishment.

I was being taken out of the game.

I wasn't seeing it for what it was because my mind was filled with lies. Lies that had seeped into my heart and kept me from knowing the truth. Lies that I accepted as truth.

Jesus had to take my red shoe wearing self over 2000 miles to pause me to listen and to truly get a hold of my heart.

And just maybe one of the many pairs of shoes I hauled clear across the country has left its mark on my sore-blistered left foot. Say nothing Engineer... say nothing!

In Max Lucado's book *3:16*[1], Max is talking about the example of Jesus:

"As a young boy, Jesus already senses the call of God. But what does he do next? Recruit apostles and preach sermons and perform miracles? No, he goes home to his folks and learns the family business. That is exactly what you should do. Want to bring focus to your life? Do what Jesus did. Go home, love your family, and take care of business."

I am a stubborn girl. I need to hear things multiple times before I truly start to listen.

God was asking me to sit, sit and be with Him.

For when we choose to hear and listen to truth, change can happen.

Slowly I was starting to hear the whispers of truth:

"You have healing to do. You are broken... and there is stuff that needs to be restored."

"For I am with you and will rescue you," declares the LORD. Jeremiah 1:8

How could someone who was a perfectionist, someone who was supposed to be in control all the time, be broken? I didn't want to be broken. This rubbed up against my pride and did not feel so good.

I am a runner, and whether I am good at it or not, I know how to do it. Just keep moving. Sitting seemed foreign to me.

I have many questions about this new position I am supposed to be taking. What is the purpose of me sitting? How long will I sit? Why am I so nervous about sitting?

In all honestly I am seeing this as a prison sentence. Go in, serve my time, get credit for good behavior and get released early. There is no ounce of me that wants to do this at all.

I am trying to sit but it only lasts for a few minutes, maybe a few days, and then I end up running again. My mind, heart and soul are not at peace. I feel nervous. A feeling that sends me out running again. The noise of the running keeps me from hearing. Running is comfortable to me. I am completely unaware of myself. Unaware of the depth of any issue.

I welcome distractions; they keep things noisy and busy.

Distractions keep me running.

When I am sitting or somewhat still, I am becoming slightly aware of a void. Not sure what it is, or why it is there. In my pride I want no one else to be aware of it.

In desperation to make the achy feeling of the void go away or lessen I 'run' to something. I stuff my face with food, go out shopping, and surround myself with people, something, anything to be in control and to drown out that feeling of 'void'. Distractions drown out the ache. I find ways to stay busy, to overschedule, to be distracted, so I am unable to hear the cries of my soul. But nothing ever seems to completely rid me of the void.

Why do I have to feel like this? I don't want to be aware of just how icky things are. What is the purpose in knowing I have this huge void and that I can't fill it, fix it or make it go away?

What is the purpose of all this? What do I need? Why can't I just get this figured out and then get on with my life? When will I get my act together?

Even though I might be sitting for a few minutes here and there, I am not listening. Nope, I am whining and complaining. "Why do I have to sit, while everyone else around me gets to run?" I argue and stubbornly keep running.

I look for distractions… maybe the phone will ring, maybe the dog will puke on the carpet, maybe I could wash the outside windows, maybe I could organize the Tupperware,

Maybe….

There is something the Creator has planned, a purpose with this whole season of sitting. It is that very something that makes me nervous. What does He want with me? What have I done wrong?

When my head hits the pillow at night right before I drift off to sleep, I am starting to hear whispers of my purpose. They are calm, peaceful whispers as to reassure me everything is going to be okay.

Be still and know I am God. Psalm 46:10

Then I wake up and I am still sitting. I don't like it here. I am not comfortable and it's definitely harder to run from this position. Try it. Sit yourself down on the floor, all the way. Now get up and run, it's not easy.

Is sitting a struggle because of pride? I don't want to miss something? Is it fear? Afraid of being lonely? Is it the fact that I didn't decide to sit and I am not in control and I really don't like that feeling very much? Do I have unrealistic expectations of others or of myself? Or maybe it's a lovely combination of all of the above! This is humbling.

How can a 30 something year old woman be in this predicament, especially one who invited Jesus into her heart in her teen years? For over twenty years I have sang the songs, attended church, read the

Bible, listened to sermons. What is missing? Is there anyone else out there who has a void?

I am starting to see I have 'issues' with pride, needing to be in control, and I am running and trying to fill a void. I am one big huge mess.

Take me away. Set me free. Closer to You.

My Prayer: I am allowing distractions to keep me from sitting and hearing. I truly am unclear right now on where You want me. Do I need rest? Do I need to be still and be taught and to hear Your voice? Help me to slow down. I know I will struggle because slow doesn't come natural to me. I know Your Word is to be still, to know who You are, trust You, and learn Your ways. Knowing in my head only gets me so far. Help Your way to sink and set into my heart, please Lord. Amen.

Fighting the Sit

In the brief moments I find myself sitting, I am fighting the process. All of my energy is focused on how to make this go faster. When am I getting up? I do not like what is happening. I am aware of a lot of negative feelings, emotions, a lot of 'yuck' is coming out of me, which makes the whole process seem even worse. I feel like a total failure, a girl who is so broken and beyond repair.

I need to heal. Just when I start to listen I get fearful and I pop up out of a sitting position and back to running again. What really needs healing anyway? I 'feel' fine. This is the mantra of my little runner self. "I feel fine!"

You can't heal what you refuse to confront.

I am frustrated, upset, disappointed, and lost. I want peace. I am sitting out here in a wilderness, my eyes have been covered and I feel like I have to figure this one out on my own. *"You got yourself into this mess Nichole, now get yourself out."* I have made dumb decisions and choices, I know that I have more to learn and that I could do with some tweaks to my character, but this is way too stinking hard. I really don't want to do this right now, actually never! I *need* a change in attitude. I am focusing on the negatives, complaining, whining, and being 'icky'. Where is joy? Where is living at peace?

I'm tired, which is so extremely hard to understand… how can I be tired while sitting? It's because I keep getting up and running. I have been chosen by Him to sit with Him and I keep running off.

But He knows the way that I take. Job 23:10a

To truly experience and live the life I was designed for, I have to be willing to leave behind my way of doing things. I have to give up control. Leave behind everything I had known, everything that feels so comfortable. A way of life I have perfected over the past 30 plus years.

I have to come completely away from the busyness, the distractions, and the noise.

I need to sit.

Sit quietly so I can hear, listen, and learn.

I have to sit.

To hear Him.

To experience Him.

To fall more in love with Him.

It's all about Him.

It's not about when I will get up.

And really it's not about what is next.

It's about the now, being in the now with Him

This is not my design. I don't get to draw the map, or call the turns. I don't know the timeline. I need to be okay with that.

While I sit, the teaching and humbling process continues.

There are moments in which this feels like eternity, a forever that will never end. Am I really that stubborn? Or is this my intended place and position?

Sitting is still quiet and lonely.

I just tucked one of my little ones into bed; the Engineer was finishing with the other. I find my book, my quilt and my oversized chair. I turn on the lamp that sits next to the chair and I start reading. I'm reading *One in a Million*[1] by Priscilla Shirer I am finding Jesus in the pages of this book. I am reading and hearing how I have to leave

Egypt, not just one foot but both feet. Both have to go. Both feet have to journey. And my eyes have to be fixed on Him, and my hand has to hold tight to His. For leaving Egypt meant I was heading into the wilderness. To sit with Him. I have to leave my way of doing things. I was very comfortable doing it all my way. My heart is learning something new. I am a Jesus loving girl and I do follow hard after Him, but I had never let Him have me completely. Why? Because I was busy running. Running for Him… I know you will start to see all the craziness of me mixed in here. It was for Him… but not fully fueled by Him. Silly how a pride control issue girl can get in the way but it happens. Leaving Egypt meant I would be leaving my way of doing things, marriage, motherhood, being a neighbor and friend, and ministry.

Marriage would be different.
Motherhood would be different.
Church would be different.
Nichole would be different.

There are so many things that can be packed into a momma's day. I have yet to ever declare I am bored. This particular day I am tackling grocery-shopping, laundry, cleaning the house and balancing school drop off and pick up and meal prep. The floors look less hairy (it's mainly from me and the girl dog), the counters feel less sticky and the overall smell of the homestead is cleaner. Well until girl dog walks by… nope! She stinks to high heaven and has to have a bath. I go pick up the boys, hurry back home, the T-Squad are at the kitchen bar eating their snack and getting started on their homework. I grab Ellie and talk, oh so sweetly to her, to coax her into the bathtub. She is not really ever super excited about the bath. I hop in the tub with her and get her smelling all good again. The after-the-bath process is what actually takes a while. I dry her with a few towels. She shakes and shakes and shakes to get the rest of the water off, which then gets hair in every nook and cranny of the bathroom. I dry her some more with a blow dryer. I open the bathroom door and she is like a prisoner being set free. She bolts out of the door and heads for the back door to be let out. I am in the process of grabbing the vacuum cleaner to de-hair the bathroom. While I am putting away the vacuum in the hall closet girl dog comes walking up to me wagging her stubby little tail and looking very happy. Wowzers… she REEKS! What in the world?! She went and rolled in something in the back yard… she must have felt too clean! Bathing the dog take two.

They prove the point of the proverbs, "A dog goes back to its own vomit" and "A scrubbed-up pig heads for the mud." 2 Peter 2:22 (The Message)

Why does Ellie Mae go in the back yard and roll in the grass to get the stink back on her? She knows the stink, and is comfortable with it. Being scrubbed up leaves her vulnerable, bare, exposed, and naked.

Change means new and different and it can be very hard and extremely uncomfortable. Going back to Egypt and living my prideful need to be in control lifestyle, was something I knew. Something that was comfortable for me.

I came so they can have real and eternal life, more and better life than they ever dreamed of. John 10:10b (The Message)

This seems out of reach for me. How do I obtain a better life? What do I have to do? It just felt too hard. I was willing to settle. Why? Was it so I could stay in control?

I am reminded of the words that Priscilla Shirer penned;

"It's easier to remain in the safety of where we've always been, doing the things we have always done. When the heavens open, when the wind of God's Spirit and the rain of His presence shower down upon us, we're uncomfortable beneath the torrent of the unfamiliar. And so we run for cover - back to the comfort zone that has kept us from really experiencing God as He now wants to be experienced.

"With His word stirring conviction within me, I prayed, 'Lord, let it rain, and give me the courage to stand under the heavens when it does. Cause me to be willing to go where You take me, even if the path is unfamiliar. Tear down any man-made religious walls that may keep me from seeing You fully. Forgive me for always running back home.' I knew He was preparing me for a new path. I needed to be open to receiving it."[2]

I refuse to go running back to Egypt to check on it, compare or keep score. I was not designed for Egypt! I need the door back to Egypt closed. There is life here in the wilderness. God is with me.

My Prayer: Thank You Lord for rescuing me out of Egypt; better still for pulling me out! Thank You Lord for placing me on this bench in this wilderness with You. Forgive me for my exits back to Egypt. Please forgive me for my lack of trust in You. I am in the wilderness… to be with You, to learn from You and to become more like You. As I feel alone out here in the wilderness I truly will keep fixed and focused on You. Knowing that I will see You, I will experience You. I pray Lord that my heart will learn from You. I pray to just be with You. Please Lord. Amen.

Benched

Over these past few months (which to a 'runner' seem like YEARS) I have been doing a whole lotta of...

Listening.
Hearing.
Healing.
Changing.
Learning.
Growing.
Maturing.

I am out here in this wilderness and I have a pretty vivid mental picture of 'sitting' on a bench. I have wanted many times to jump right up off this bench and go back to running. I know how to run. I know how to go and do. You would think the longer I sit on this bench the more comfortable I would get. Nope. There is still something inside that wants to jump up and get back in the game. And so I ask many times...

"Am I ready yet?"
"Have we done enough?"
"Am I healed and all better?"
Some of those questions get louder and louder and I find myself

asking them more often when the days are lonely, long and hard. Or when I see others running…

Being benched is not getting to play in the game. It is having to watch others do what you want to be doing.

I beg to get up; I plead to get up. I barter to sit for a while with breaks for good behavior. You may think I am kidding or making this stuff up, and believe me I wish I was. How embarrassing is it that a grown woman can't sit and obey.

I look for anything to build my case that I have served my time and I am done sitting.

Thursday night I shared with The Engineer how I felt his schedule was too much and how I was getting tired. I definitely was whining and complaining. I wanted to hear him say, *"Oh you are right Nichole I need to stop everything and just focus on you and the family."* But what he really said was, "I need you to support me right now". I wanted to scream! I felt so disconnected from him, and thought, *"Where is the man I married?"* *"Where is the man who would do anything for me?"*

So, after a goodnight's sleep and a little perspective shift I realized I was trying to get The Engineer to let me off the bench. I was working a different angle. How embarrassing! But I have to be completely honest. I am obviously not embracing this whole sitting thing if I am still trying to get off the bench. I have tried using the people in my life to 'free' me of this horrible sentence I have been given. I just know that someone will utter the words that will free me. The bad news is I can't find a soul who will release me from this no fun 'icky' sitting season. At some point I will run out of angles to try, right? I so want to get this. And just now as I type these words I hear in my heart, "Nichole it's not about 'getting anything' it's about trusting Me, focusing on Me, loving Me, being with Me."

I am brave enough to go and share this whole thing with my Pastor. I just know he will hear this craziness and inform me I most surely am NOT hearing from God and that I have created this whole silly thing on my own. I just know he will say, *"Nichole you are free to go."* I finished telling Pastor Mike what is going on and he responded, "This really does sound like a God thing Nichole."

What? Are you serious? I must not be hearing him right!

There is no one, not a single person who doesn't think this is where I am supposed to be. People who I do life with know me; they know I am not a 'sitter'. Also people who know God realize that many times He asks us to do things that are not in our girly red shoe wearing nature to do on our own.

No matter where my ears tune in, or my eyes read, everything I take in keeps confirming I am to be sitting.

Sitting is so quiet. In the quiet I hear and sense all that is not 'right' with me, even while my mind, heart and soul fight this, I am being surrounded, encircled by constant confirmation that I need this time to be healed. I need to sit.

Just plain ole sitting.

I enjoy people. I enjoy seeing them, hearing about all their stories, living vicariously through them as they go on vacations. I truly enjoy people. Being out here in 'this place' gets lonely. As I sit on this bench I can see space on either side of me. In my flesh I desire for someone to be sitting on the bench with me, another human, and this morning I truly sense You saying, "No Nichole, that space is for MORE of Me."

Now don't get me wrong I know God is with me. I am not trying to be disrespectful or in any way dishonor Him. But in my humanness I am lonely.

Loneliness is so not my thing.

To whom He said, 'This is the resting place, let the weary rest'; and, 'This is the place of repose.' Isaiah 28:12

I want to be on the go. In the limelight. On the stage. Hanging with the people. Hearing the noise. He wants me sitting. In the quiet. On the bench. Hanging with Him. Hearing His voice.

The Engineer and I talk about my need to be still, to obey and embrace this time on the bench. The Engineer encourages me to seek contentment and be with God. I shed a lot of tears last night that held fear, worry, and confusion. I even had to let go of my visions and dreams, because I knew I was holding onto those more than I was holding onto what God had for me. I do want to rest in Him on this bench. I want to know Him more. I want to learn from Him. I want to embrace sitting on the bench.

I am sitting far back on this bench, my shoes are off and I am trying to embrace this. I am aware of much more when I am resting. I am more aware of things that are not right and need healing.

I am learning that my captivity, that which imprisons me, is my pride, my people pleasing, my anxious worried thoughts, my control issues and my fear of the unknown.

Why? Why are these my character traits?

Why can't I just be 'good'?

You can just open that big ole book called the Bible to any ole page and start reading. I have tried it many times. Kind of like a last minute cry for help. I quickly flip open the pages,

I've opened to Psalm 145 and the subtitle in my Bible reads:

Because God is full of love, He satisfies all who trust in Him.

Desperately needing help and answers I start reading.

I read and re-read those words over and over. I want this love, I want to be satisfied, but I question, "Can I fully trust Him?"; "Am I good enough for this love?"

I have noticed I tend to be okay with this whole sitting thing when it's just between God and me. But when these moments leave the comfort of my home and come out amongst others, then pride decides to show its ugly self.

I am not comfortable with everyone seeing me sit.

Will my head and heart ever reside within the same body? There seems to be a disconnection. There is no peace between the two. My head continues to entertain the negative thoughts, the lies, the worry, the anxiety, the need to control, and the desire to do better. If I could just earn my way! If I could just be better and get this figured out maybe then my heart and head would be at peace. My head is full of chaos. Not peaceful, not calm. My head has a standard that my heart was never created to live at. Where does that standard come from? Have I created it?

There seems to be a lot of cleaning up, fixing, and healing that needs to be done in my life. How in the world can I accomplish this and be a wife and mom at the same time? It would be much easier if this could all just take place in my walk in closet, away from an audience. You see people like me, who want to be in control and have pride issues, we don't like to be in front of people until everything is all in order and presentable.

There are days I am slowing down and don't find myself running full speed ahead, rather sitting at His feet, trying to allow His peace and calmness to surround me. I am starting to see things differently. My heartbeat is starting to beat slower.

I am sitting. I would like to say I put myself here because that would be a good Christian girl answer, but I didn't. I have been sat down. Humbled. Not punished. Humbled. Sat down so I can listen and learn.

I can see the lack of balance in my life.

I find myself not somewhere I would have taken myself, but oddly enough it's where I am supposed to be.

I am wondering what my purpose is. What was I created for?

If it's not running, striving and doing, then what?

So what do I do next?

So roll up your sleeves, put your mind in gear, be totally ready to receive the gift that's coming when Jesus arrives. Don't lazily slip back into those old grooves of evil, doing just what you feel like doing. You didn't know any better then; you do now. As obedient children, let yourselves be pulled into a way of life shaped by God's life, a life energetic and blazing with holiness. God said, "I am holy; you be holy."

You call out to God for help and he helps—he's a good Father that way. But don't forget, he's also a responsible Father, and won't let you get by with sloppy living.

Your life is a journey you must travel with a deep consciousness of God. It cost God plenty to get you out of that dead-end, empty-headed life you grew up in. He paid with Christ's sacred blood, you know. He died like an unblemished, sacrificial lamb. And this was no afterthought. Even though it has only lately—at the end of the ages—become public knowledge, God always knew he was going to do this for you. It's because of this sacrificed Messiah, whom God then raised from the dead and glorified, that you trust God, that you know you have a future in God. 1 Peter 1:13-21 (The Message)

The words I focus on;
God says, "I am holy; you be holy."
Just be? Be holy? Yeah right! With my past, my thoughts, my propensity to say things without filtering them. How in the world is a girl like me to be holy?
What am I to **do**?

My Prayer: May I know that loneliness on this journey is only a matter of earthly perception. The God of the Universe, my Creator You are with me every minute. Make my mind, heart and soul be fixed on You. You are in every moment with me. May I realize I am not being punished but rather experiencing You. Help me to focus on the here and now… this moment. You are for me. You save, heal, redeem and love completely. Lord, help me to 'sit' and to allow You to do Your thing. Amen.

Sitting on the Porch

The Engineer, as I refer to my best friend and husband, does life in a matter of fact way, most of the 24 hours of the day. If he sees an issue then he solves it. Me, his wife of 18 plus years, has quite a few more feelings and emotions about things. I tend to see more grey in the spectrum than he does.

The Engineer and I are sitting on the back porch and I am stressing, worrying, and questioning my position and purpose in life. I start word vomiting out everything that comes to my mind (a bad habit I have when I need relief from the stress of the millions of thoughts running through my mind). I am hypothetically asking, "What am I supposed to do now, now that I am just sitting?" I think it's called a rhetorical question. HA! I was NOT asking the Engineer to solve anything. Just listen. But nope he didn't. And matter of factly declared these words;

"You write a book."

They are delivered from The Engineer's mouth as the 'fix all' to my life's problems. They fall on hard of hearing ears, and a stubborn and prideful heart.

What? I think I went into shock. I started fighting against those words… **I can't write**. I remember how I struggled in all of my English classes. I still have no proof that I attended them. I have vivid memories of red ink, and instructors shaking their heads. I don't use the right words let alone in the right order, and then to throw some punctuation in there. Seriously? Write a book? I want to grab those words out of the air and shove them back down into the Engineer's throat. Not for a second will I spend anytime hearing them. I will not let them anywhere near my mind or heart.

So now you can blame the Engineer for all this!

What I want to do right now is go for a run. Get off this back porch, out of the house and go for a run. But instead I get in the car and go run some errands.

I am alone in my car driving and I throw up the silly and insane idea of writing a book to God. "Can you even believe how crazy the Engineer's latest idea is?"

"This commandment that I'm commanding you today isn't too much for you, it's not out of your reach. It's not on a high mountain — you don't have to get mountaineers to climb the peak and bring it down to your level and explain it before you can live it. And it's not across the ocean —you don't have to send sailors out to get it, bring it back, and then explain it before you can live it. No. The word is right here and now — as near as the tongue in your mouth, as near as the heart in your chest. Just do it!" Deuteronomy 30:11-14 (The Message).

God's response was SO not what I expected. He confirmed that the idea was not the Engineer's, He just chose to use the Engineer to deliver the message.

I blurt out my defending argument, "This is so out of character for me, I am NOT a writer!"

I am NOT Max Lucado, A.W. Tozer, Eugene Peterson, Joyce Meyer, Beth Moore, Jen Hatmaker, Lysa Terkeurst. Seriously, "What are You thinking Lord?"

And then calmly I hear:

"I didn't call you to be a writer, I asked you to sit down and write." What?

Is there a difference? And again I hear it repeated...

"I didn't call you to be a writer, I asked you to sit down and write."

I don't know many big fancy words. And sometimes I use the wrong words, ask the Engineer, or my girlfriends who go on walks late at night with me. I have good intentions, but I learned last night that 'shank and flank' have different meanings and are not interchangeable with each other.

Writing is easy. All you have to do is cross out the wrong words.[1] ~ Mark Twain

As I am driving in my little Subaru Outback, God goes on to inform me that the book has a title, *'Do You Know I Love You?'* I am repeating this title over and over in my brain. I know I am not getting the full impact of its meaning. But I do know I have heard this question a bunch of times. The Engineer has asked me for years, "Do You Know I Love You?" But as I sit here at this stoplight waiting to go, I am held in this moment, there is something more to this question. For it originates not with The Engineer.

Where does one officially start writing a book? Introduction? Recently the Engineer introduced our son Tyler to 'choose your own adventure books' and when it's my turn to read with him at night I have been thinking… *"Hey that's what this book writing adventure feels like as it unfolds."* Random writing but unsure of how to organize it all? The word organize scares me. No worries you won't have to flip to different pages, but know that I did entertain the idea… as that would keep this whole writing thing fun!

"Nichole let Me lead. Let Me guide this process. I know that you have been stressing and worrying about this whole book thing… and I don't want you to. I want you to know that I will do what needs to be done. You just write from your heart. Write what you hear, what you experience, what you feel. I will put it all together, because I love you Nichole."- God

Put no confidence in the flesh. Philippians 3:3

My Prayer: Lord I have no confidence in myself to write this book. This honestly feels so hard and I feel so weak. I am nothing in my flesh. There is no strength or ability in me. Why have I tried for years to do it all on my own? Without You I can do nothing. Help me to realize this. Amen.

Learn to Be Still

Sitting on the back porch hearing The Engineer say the words "You write a book" was so crazy for me… one that it was him encouraging me to do it, and second that it was something that seemed so out of character for me. I can't write. Seriously? Write a book?

I am sitting here typing in a file that I titled 'Book Journal' and I am scared. These past few months have been such an adjustment. I don't find myself running so far out ahead now. Rather I am sitting, or better yet, learning to be still. It's where He invited me to be.

The LORD your God is with you, He is mighty to save. He
will take great delight in you, He will quiet you with His love,
He will rejoice over you with singing. Zephaniah 3:17

I am a few weeks out from hearing about this whole book idea that I am supposed to write. I am starting to sense that the question in the book title, *'Do You Know I Love You?'* corresponds with the void I am faintly aware of deep in my soul. Maybe He, God, my Creator has been pursuing me for years… all these years while I have been running, asking me this question, "Do You Know I Love You?" Maybe I am sitting because I need to hear it.

Have you ever had one of those moments where you realize something and you think, *"I bet everyone else around me already knows this, but me?"* There is no positive feeling in that, rather embarrassment and shame. Well at least there is for me. I am struggling - yes I know it's a pride thing. But the truth is I don't want to be the last one to learn life's sometimes difficult lessons!

I am a whole lot of nervous right now. I am at my laptop trying and/or pretending to write a book. Why am I nervous? Because I am uncomfortable. Because it again confirms the whole 'sit' season. It means I must sit still, be away from people and be by myself. I must take the time. I am nervous, confused and overwhelmed. I am a mess!

I can't guarantee the content of the pages of this book. Just typing out that little 11 - word sentence scares me more than a 'tad'. For girls like me who like to be in control, the unknowns simply go against our human nature. I will be sharing the journey of a girl, who for many years was busy 'doing'. She didn't know how to be still. I am going to try my hardest to type in first person, however in all honesty third person feels more comfortable and safer. Who doesn't want to be comfortable and safe? I know I sure do!

The Engineer starts playing *Learn to be Still[1]* by the Eagles on his guitar;

He starts to sing the words.

I find myself wanting the chaos in my head to be silenced.

I have 'run' for years to find happiness.

I want to be satisfied.

But it's more comfortable to keep running.

My friend informed me she was part of a running group and if I ever wanted to join in I could. The group was made up of working moms, women yet to be moms, stay at home moms, moms with kids in all seasons of life and the common denominator was running. The group rightly named themselves, *Runner Girls,* and they would run together throughout the week for training runs, sign up for races together, and most importantly do life together.

I had been invited many times to go on a run with the Runner

Girls. But in my 'pride' I kept declining. I wasn't ready to run with them yet. I was more of a shuffle, breathe deep and whine my way through the run kinda gal. The Runner Girls were the real thing, Garmin watches, no walk breaks, knock out five miles and be home before the family wakes for the morning. I was around the three mile mark. And felt very proud of that. Five miles was way too far. That was for runners. But one morning I woke at 4:15am. Who in their right mind gets up at that crazy hour? Only runners, but here I am putting on my shorts, running shoes and meeting up with the Runner Girls for my initiation run. I was going to pretend to do this! Call it half asleep, mixed with the prideful stubborn girl that I am but I ran 5.18 miles with the Runner Girls. I did it! And that included a pretty significant hill too. Now granted, I did have my very own personal cheerleaders running alongside me at various points in the run. But I did it - 5.18 miles.

The irony of becoming a 'runner' during a season that God has called me to be still and sit is so hard for me to wrap my little brain around.

So hard that yesterday I wanted to fix the pain, the hurt, I wanted to flee the doubts, worry, and questions. I wanted to run. I chose to sit.

God is within her, she will not fall; God will help her at break of day. Psalm 46:5

I don't want to be running around without purpose and just 'doing' stuff. However, this 'sitting' seems so 'slow'. I am struggling because this is not my normal pace. I know I am supposed to be still, know and trust God. I know! I know! I do know. Knowing in my head only gets me so far. I need it to work its way into my heart.

My heart feels the pain and struggle of the continual shifting and changing. It is unsettling and uncomfortable and purposeful and right all at the same time.

The LORD Almighty is with us. Psalm 46:11

The One, asking me to pause. Asking me to sit.

Needing me to wait. Wanting me to hear Him.

I am afraid to see and hear all that is not good and not right with me. All the reasons that I could not and should not be loved. Whoa… that's a big ole statement, one that took a whole lot of guts to throw out there for you to read. But I state it because it's part of the healing process for me. If one believes they shouldn't be, then they find many supporting reasons to make that true. If I am not good enough for love I will find the 'facts' to make that statement true.

The LORD will fight for you; you need only to be still. Exodus 14:14

Why am I still dealing with these issues in my 30's? How embarrassing! Maybe it's because in the moments I did slow down I never paused long enough. When I did pause, the stuff was just all too much for me, the hurt, the 'yuck'. I really didn't want to sort through the stuff and most definitely didn't want to deal with it.

My Prayer: As the sun is coming up I am reminded of this new day. A day in which You have written and the story and song sings out in heaven already. I want to be still and know You are God. The colors of the sunrise that are peeking in through my bedroom curtains are reminding me I have truly only seen a glimpse of who You are. And that someday I will see You in all Your fullness for eternity. Oh what a day that will be, to fall down at Your feet and to thank You for all Your precious patience with me. To say I love You. To wrap my little frail tired weary arms around Your big mighty strength filled enduring being and hold this moment for eternity. I love You Lord, Amen.

Being vs Doing

Doing is comfortable and safe for me, and I think I am good at it. For years I chose 'doing', to the point of unhealthy. To the point of addiction. But now that I am siting more I can look back and see that many times over the years I would get stopped and made to rest, to pause, to be still. And every time I fought it. Every time! There has always been something I didn't like about being still. What did I fear would happen in those quiet and still moments?

There were a few moments that added up in my twenties that made me realize I was truly missing out on something. I was tired of going through the motions, being the good girl, and just following the rules.

This morning I wake and read Galatians 5 in The Message Bible. Paul is encouraging the Galatians to not focus on the law. The law can't save them. He reminds them that the focus shouldn't be on the law and all the rules to follow, but rather to follow after Jesus. In the shower just now I was thinking about the 'rule' to only wear white after Memorial Day and before Labor Day. To be honest I am not sure if I even have the 'rule' correct, as I don't follow it. I tend to be allergic to some rules. HA! No really, think about all the rules you hear and know. Truly think about them. So many of them are just absolutely silly. Really if I want to wear white who is it bothering or offending? Why am I so passionate about this whole rule thing? I think because for so long I lived by the rules. I tried to find more rules to follow so as to impress

God. "Look at me, I am following all the rules." And when things went bad or wrong then I would question Him, "Why is this happening to me? Me of all people? I am following all the rules!"

Am I a Jesus follower or a rule and law follower?

If such is the case, is the law, then, an anti-promise, a negation of God's will for us? Not at all. Its purpose was to make obvious to everyone that we are, in ourselves, out of right relationship with God, and therefore to show us the futility of devising some religious system for getting by our own efforts what we can only get by waiting in faith for God to complete his promise. For if any kind of rule-keeping had power to create life in us, we would certainly have gotten it by this time. Galatians 3:21-22 (The Message).

So trying to be a 'good girl' is too hard and too much work. I want the relationship not the religion.

Many Israelites walking around in the wilderness had religion mastered.

I am in the middle of the wilderness sitting on the bench and if it's not to learn and follow all the rules, what am I to be doing?

I am a girl who likes to do things my way.

Well, it has been brought to my attention most recently that 'my way' is not going to work anymore. It is the main reason I have found myself out here in this wilderness… sitting with God. But kudos to me for sitting long enough to hear Him.

I am tired of doing it my way. As I sit out here on the bench I can hear Him saying… "Nichole there is only one-way. My way. I am The Way."

It hits me that I am NOT in the wilderness to identify all the tree species. I am NOT in the wilderness to create the best campfire dinner. I am NOT in the wilderness to critique the journey of all the other wilderness travelers.

The purpose of the wilderness is:
- To hear Him.
- To experience Him.
- To fall more in love with Him.
- It's all about Him.
- It's not about pitchin' a tent or a fit.
- It's not about when I will get out.
- And really it's not about what is next.
- It's about the now, being in the now with Him.
- The wilderness is not my design. I don't get to draw the map, or call the turns. I don't know the timeline. And I really need to be okay with that.
- When I allow Him to bring me completely out of Egypt, and allow Him to wrap me in His love, and trust that He has great things for me then I will walk peacefully with Him through the wilderness.

More than anything I want to be the daughter, wife, mom, sister, and friend He created me to be. And for years I have tried. I have tried to 'do' all that, and you know - I am hearing Him say that I was trying to do it my way.

So as I sit here on this bench I have been asking;

"How then God can I do it Your way?"

"Come," - He replied, "and you will see." John 1:39

Some days, are long, hard and very overwhelming.

I am thinking about not 'trying' today.

Which goes against everything inside of me.

Seriously.

If you could see my heart beating or take my blood pressure right now... you would know I am a little worked up about it... a little apprehensive to say the least.

Something I read this morning has me thinking about 'not trying' today.

*It does not, therefore, depend on man's desire or effort,
but on God's mercy. Romans 9:16*

I cannot save myself. There is NO amount of 'trying' that will make this happen. There is NO amount of tap dancing, twirling, or earning that will make God reach down and determine that now is the time I deserve to be saved, loved, healed and restored!

For it has nothing to do with me.

It's all about Him.

His mercy.

May I stop trying and let it be.

I am thinking about *doing vs being*. How our human heart is tuned to **do**, and how our God redeemed heart, a heart that has been changed by our Savior is allowed to **be**. This is a daily struggle for me.

Learning to be. Be. A two letter word with a whole lot of meaning. Be loved. Be still. Be content. Be patient. Be willing.

Be present in the situation you are in. Be aware of where God has you. Be participating. Be seeking Him. Be grateful and thankful for all He has done.

Romans 10 (Have I mentioned how much I LOVE the book of Romans?!)

*That if you confess with your mouth, 'Jesus is Lord' and believe in
your heart that God raised Him from the dead, you will be saved.
For it is with your heart that you believe and are justified, and it
is with your mouth that you confess and are saved. (v9-10)*

For, Everyone who calls on the name of the Lord, will be saved. (v13)

Help me Lord to NOT make it more than what You have said it to be. You have stated it simply. Help me keep it simple!

I am asking, "What do you want me to do?"

God answers, "I want you to **be** loved."

In my fleshly nature I feel compelled to always be doing something. To prove my worth, to earn acceptance, to make others like and love me. I have mastered doing. Being comes much harder for me.

Being

[**bee**-ing] /ˈbi ɪŋ/

noun

1. the fact of existing; existence

But just as He who called you is holy, so be holy in all you do; for it is written: 'Be holy, because I am holy'. 1 Peter 1:15-16

There it is again. The whole *'be holy'* thing! I have learned with God that He will keep repeating Himself as I am hard to get through to.

Be Holy. Created to be. Be versus Do. We weren't created to 'do' holy… Bible reading, praying, church attending. Our design is to 'be' in relationship with Him. Being in relationship with the One. The One who created us to 'be'.

"Am I doing enough?" "Am I spending enough time with God?"

I will never feel like I have 'done' enough. I wasn't created to be a doer.

There are moments in which I find myself being humbled at the feet of Jesus much faster than in the past. And I praise God for that change and progress… because it's a sign that God is working in me.

*To **be** overcome by Your presence, Lord.*[2]

'Being' is God's design, and thus does not jive with the worlds trends. Think of our society. The busyness of schedules. The organization, planning, scheduling. There are so many imbalances in our society to the point of unhealthy people and unhealthy families. Why is there no time to just 'be'? For us to know and hear Love we need to stop running from it and chasing after it. We need to seek to be. To be loved.

One of my favorite times of the day is 'being' at our dining room table and eating a meal together as a family. I sit across from The Engineer and next to each one of my boys. Being at the table. Team Hamblin being together. Sharing yummy food. Chatting about our day. Being.

My Prayer: Please remove the bondage of my own fleshly convictions. May I humble myself to Your plan and know ultimately it will bring me closer to you. To be in relationship with, You, my Creator. Daily. Moment by moment aware of Your Presence. Here with me. Loving me. Lord, strengthen me to stay. Stay here in this moment. Not rushing ahead or dwelling on what was. Here in this moment. Aware of You. Aware of You and who You are. All of You. Thank You for Your patience with me. Thank You for teaching me You are not limited. You are not contained. May I remain here with You. Here aware of You. Breathing in and out with purpose. How sweet is that, I love You-Amen.

Let It All Go

The book. I can't get out of it any longer! I have thrown out all the excuses, I am not a writer, I can't do it, and there are other people who are more qualified. I am hoping to be released from this. I am so stinkin' nervous. I am easily distracted. I have been putting off writing this book for a few days. Okay a lotta few days. Who is counting? Okay maybe someone is counting, but He has been super-duper patient with me.

I started the project I was asked to do. And friends I have no clue… NO CLUE what I am doing. I am NOT a writer. I am a girl who likes to communicate… but not in proper complete sentences. I rush to get ideas out, and I always process out loud and then realize I probably didn't need to share all that. So this makes me so stinkin' nervous.

Write a book. Those three words make me feel all sorts of weird emotions. I can't - I can't write a book. I don't know what I am doing. I am scared beyond all levels of scared. Here I am on this very uncomfortable chair in front of my laptop and my head is full of negatives like- *"Someone else could write this book better than you. You have never written a book before. Writers know how to form sentences. Who will even read this book?"* I am struggling with this whole *'writing'* thing. The bigness of this project is so overwhelming. I feel like I am not good 'enough' for this. What do I focus on? Where in the world do I start? I search up (The Engineer and the T-Squad love that phrase of mine) biblegateway.com and type in the search box **love**… 698 verses on love. I start to read… and my spirit quietens and becomes calm. I sense His presence. I think I have a lot to learn. May I not have my own words.

Fill your paper with the breathings of your heart.[1] ~William Wordsworth

I have read Numbers 11 this morning and it delivered a huge gut punch. The Israelites are whining and complaining about eating 'only manna'. They are sick and tired of this white stuff that falls from the sky each day to feed and nourish them. They miss the delicacies of what was on their plates in Egypt. I can relate. I am missing the things that make me feel more comfortable. Hanging out with people, buying shoes, filling voids, distracting myself. I miss Egypt. I crave those things. I know those things. I feel uncomfortable without them. I want to know in my heart that craving God is what I was designed to do, meant for. I feel like this is all way TOO MUCH for me. Too hard. Too restrained. Too foreign. Too lonely. Too submissive. Too servant oriented. I know as I type some of the above it's hard for me as a 'Jesus and people pleasing girl' to see… but it's the honest truth.

Psalm 78 is stirring in my mind, heart and soul.

They willfully put God to the test by demanding the food they craved. (v18)

I am guilty of telling God just what I need to be happy. I am guilty of testing God. Testing to see if He will give up on me and walk away.

*They ate till they had more than enough, for he had
given them what they craved. (v29)*

I have had enough of my way. I know I need to step aside and allow God to love me. I know I need to trust Him and His way.

Yet he was merciful; he forgave their iniquities and did not destroy them. (v38)

Exodus 23:20-33 personalized for me;

"Look Nichole I have sent an angel before you, to guard you along the way and to bring you to the place I have prepared. Pay attention and listen. Do not rebel, do not whine; do not disobey. My name is in the angel. If you listen carefully to what he says and do all that I say, I will be an enemy to your enemies and will oppose those who oppose you. My angel will go ahead of you and bring you into the land of the 'ites', the land I have promised you, and I will wipe out the 'ites' for you. 'Ites' being selfishness, pride, thoughts, stubbornness, control issues, people pleasing issues, greed, bitterness, unforgivness, fear. I will wipe them out! Do not bow down before their gods or worship them or follow their practices. Turn Nichole from your old way of filling voids, don't pay attention to the things of this world, don't worry about what others think, say or do, don't give into the world's way of dealing with life, I want you Nichole to do it My way. Nichole you must demolish these gods in your life, demolish them and break their sacred stones to pieces. You must be done and rid of them and the bondage they are keeping you in. Nichole, worship Me and My blessing will be on your food and water. Nichole, focus on Me, think about Me, spend time with Me and I will bless you, I will take care of you. I will make you all I need you to be. I will heal you. I will provide for you, I will protect you. And Nichole your ministry the one I created you to live out, will not 'miscarry or be barren' I will give you a full life span. I will send My terror ahead of you and throw into confusion every nation you encounter. Nichole I have this, I can handle anything that comes at you. I will make all your enemies turn their backs and run; temptation, fear, worry, doubt, pride, selfishness, control, they will not be your way! I will send the hornet ahead of you to drive these things out of you and your path. But I will not do it in a single year because it's not My way, and it would be too much for you. Little by little I will drive them out before you, until you have increased enough to take possession of the land. Until you are built strong and ready for the ministry I have created you for. I, Nichole will establish for you borders, guidelines, regulations that are created just for you

with mercy, grace and love to live life abundantly in. Nichole, don't settle for any less, but choose Nichole to do it My way. Do not make a covenant with them or with their gods. Do not let them live in your land, or they will cause you to sin against me, because the worship of their gods will certainly be a snare to you."

I realize my whining, complaining, and missing my old ways hurts God's heart. I have taken my eyes off Him. I am craving Egypt. I am making this process harder on myself.

"Daughter it has to go. The self-first thoughts. The need to control. The need to want your way, it's all got to go!"

About a week ago I was running and was headed up this pretty significant hill, and I was tired, sweaty, and had lost all my running mates. I had somehow gotten off the course and I was ready to be done. All of sudden I said out loud, "Okay God I will be the movement, but You have to supply the strength!" And sure enough I found myself at the end of this run. I had accidentally run 10 miles!

This morning in the shower I am boldly reminded that *'a book will not write itself'*.

So I update my FB status: "It's a writing day and I am SCARED to death... please just pray that I will be a good girl and 'just do it', I am easily distracted." And my momma comments: "God has already written it... just hold on to the pencil."   Those words sent from above to this desperate, scared and needy heart.

I am out on a training run this morning. The Runner Girls talked me into running my first half marathon. What in the heck was I thinking? I'm running solo this morning so I am alone with my thoughts. Thoughts of sending both my boys to school. An upcoming hysterectomy surgery that is a must. A half marathon. I can't even. As I turn to head back home the sunrise is so amazing. It's coloring the sky. The sky is a bright yellow and orange and pink. It's beautiful. It's heaven reaching down into the middle of the chaos and stress. A beautiful interruption.

I want to stay in the closet until,
- My hormones, feelings, thoughts don't rule my behaviour.
- My face doesn't break out.
- My belly is flat.
- I can play well with others.
- I am not easily distracted by stuff and things.
- I don't fill voids with the wrong things.
- I can be a good mommy.
- I am not overwhelmed.
- I am healed.
- I am the girl that He originally designed me to be.
- I don't whine, complain, worry, doubt.
- I am not afraid.
- I think more of Him and less of me.
- I can be the wife the Engineer needs.
- I am filled with Him.
- I am ready.

I like my closet. There's room for me and not much more.

It's literally a walk in closet; you just walk in and stand there. Sitting works well too. I have found that with the door closed and the lights out, all is quiet, and comfortable. I don't have to 'deal' with stuff on the other side of the door. It's safe. Things seem less hard in the closet. I don't get things wrong. I don't say the wrong things. I am begging my Jesus to explain to me why in the world do I have to do it His way. For He wants me to live life on purpose out amongst people. That is too hard. People can see my mistakes, my flaws, my 'owies', and my hurts. I have never felt more naked. They are seeing me struggle and fail. It's hurting my pride.

Inside the closet I feel more secure, more in control, less in a fog. My way seems so much easier.

Easier on me!

Can't Jesus just fix me, heal me, restore me, do whatever He needs to do and then when I am ready open the closet door and let me out?

Because really I prefer to stay in the closet, thanks!

In the quietness of the closet I can hear Him whisper,

"Daughter will you trust me? Will you dare to believe me? I do all that I do in love. Love for you. Come on out of the closet Nichole, its okay. For you are thinking others will see your nakedness, but that's where you are wrong. They won't see you, they will see Me. The living graceful, passionate love of Jesus… ready to love on them. You are just the 'one' I will be using to display all of that. So please get out of the way and allow Me to do it, because people need to know that I love them. Thank you, Nichole, Sincerely God."

This house is insanely quiet. It is all I can do to sit here. The life, the energy, the noise is gone. It makes this whole season of sitting that much harder. And He knew. He knew that I would have to share both of the boys with the local elementary school. That for 6 1/2 hours each day a piece of my heart would be located a mile down the road from our homestead. That I would be sitting here with me, myself and I.

They will turn to the LORD, and He will respond to
their pleas and heal them. Isaiah 19:22b

I need to sit, and I need to be changed by God, the only One who can do it right, completely, and create the much needed result. The healing and restoration of my heart, mind, body and soul. I pray for a realization of this in my humanness NOT to beat myself down, but to carry myself to Him and ask for help, ask for strength to keep going, ask for the right words and actions.

It's pouring down rain this morning. The morning I am going to go out and run 13.1 miles. I think I am prepared physically for my first half marathon. I have run the miles. It's the mental aspect that I am most concerned about. Me, my thoughts and I do usually like to spend time together. Running this far with your thoughts can get a tad overwhelming. I will be running will some of the best Runner Girls ever. They will keep me from 'thinking' too much. I had to beg my surgeon to schedule my hysterectomy around this race. I had to get this in. I know after my surgery I will have to take a few weeks off to heal and recover. More resting and sitting still!

The hardest part of my first half marathon was staying focused on my race. I found myself concerned at who was running faster, who was making it up the hills better, who wasn't taking walking breaks. Why did that old man make it across the finish line before me? I finished, but wish I had mentally finished stronger.

Having a hysterectomy in your 30's was not part of my life plan. But life doesn't always go, as we would like it to. I was looking forward to not dealing with the endometriosis and ovarian cysts. However the fear of the unknown on the other side! What would my hormones be like? What was menopause in my 30's going to be like? I was going to have to rest and let my body heal. I was going to have to allow others to help with meals, clean the house, care for the boys. There were a lot of unknowns coming. I wasn't in control.

"Trust Me Nichole. Take the time. Don't rush this. You deserve to be healed completely. Your heart, mind and soul need to be completely healed. Your body will follow suit. I love You Nichole, don't let go of My hand. I have got You."-God

I am lonely. I need this time I know it was 'scheduled'. All this time to be thinking! I am scared of this no hormone thing and what will happen with my body and my emotions. There is so much changing. To add to it I need to clean out my closet. Literally. It's a mess. There is so much crammed in there. I don't even know how I find stuff to wear. There are things that have to go. But I am scared to clean out my closet. I am not good at letting things go.

I had put it off for three days... the cleaning out of my closet. I knew there were a few items that just had to go because they were too big. However, the actual task of doing it was overwhelming and I wasn't sure why. Tuesday night I had told The Engineer, "It's easier to clean out someone else's closet" and that is when God started to speak so loud ... "Of course it is Nichole, but I don't want you dealing with the specks in everyone else's life I want you to deal with the logs in your own." So I call my girlfriend and whine and complain and tell her I was struggling. What does she do? She jumps in her car and shows up at my door. She instructs me to come in the bed room and take a seat. She takes each item out of my dresser drawers and has me decide to keep it, toss it or donate it. Then repeats the process with my closet. There emerged a large pile on the bed and an even larger pile in the closet doorway. Clothes I was fighting to give up, justified in keeping. Clothes that were old, worn out, too big, and stained. There were so many empty hangers when she was done. The closet is open, airy, has space. There were great clothes left and yet I felt completely naked!

The experience was so embarrassing. Trash bags full of stuff. Stuff the enemy said I needed to cover up and hide, to keep people from seeing the real me. Clothes that were being thrown out that didn't make me feel good, but I had them for protection. What if I needed them? What if the lack of hormones caused me to gain a bunch of weight and I needed the clothes again? The pile in the doorway of the closet was a huge representation of the enemy keeping me from what God has for me. Cleaning out the closet was emotionally hard and it hurt. It hurts to be exposed and naked. My girlfriend left the house with the bags of clothes that had to go. She showed back up at my house with new pajamas. I felt so undeserving. So humbled. So exposed. So needy! Do I deserve it? Am I worth it?

I am trying to be obedient and follow the directions of *'rest and heal'*, which sounds an awful like 'sitting' to me. This morning my Jesus reminded me...

*The thief comes only to steal and kill and destroy; I have come
that they may have life, and have it to the full. John 10:10*

The thief is Satan, the enemy, and he is sitting close trying to throw
me off course. He wants me to feel pathetic, miserable, full of yuck.
The enemy reminds me I am barely able to move around, while my
friends are out running. The enemy wants me to remember right now
I can't be the wife and mom I want to be, while others are cooking and
taking care of my family. The enemy wants to point out that I can't
wear jeans and am stuck wearing yoga pants because of my swollen
belly. Oh and we won't mention the lack of attention my hair is getting!

Humbled. Exposed. Bare. There is so much that can be entangled
and wrapped around us, and so much that can be stuffed in us, that
being stripped and made bare is cleansing and healing.

I am looking at that yuck, feeling ashamed, disappointed and guilty.
I need help in remembering this is part of the process. This stuff has to
go out of my life; it is ugly and not fitting for me. It is NOT what God
designed for me to be dressed in.

I have to let it all go and know these are the things I can do without.

My Prayer: I want to know the full extent of Your love. Why am
I fighting You? Why? Lord I need You to break me of this struggle.
For I see the yuck and smell the stink of what is coming off and
being removed, but my hope is that people see You. Clean me
of the things that are keeping me from fully experiencing You. I
pray for the yuck that has to go - bitterness, pride, jealousy, worry,
doubt, fear, lack of patience, lack of self-control, selfishness. I need
Your presence. I need You to be my everything. Help me to know.
Help me to accept. Remove that which blocks the knowing and the
accepting. Please Lord. Amen.

The Void

One of the things I have struggled with in this whole process is that it feels so raw, bare, naked, exposed to be doing all this healing while still having to do life. For there is purpose in the exposure. Pride says, "No thank you I don't want people to see me naked."

It is present in each of our souls. It can manifest in many ways to get our attention. The void. Mine manifested in a great desire to be liked, appreciated, and most importantly loved. For years I have tried to fill the void with relationships, my career, eating, shoe shopping. Most recently running. Nothing ever completely filled the void. For it led to disappointment. Unmet expectations. 'Owies' time and time again. Loneliness, hurt, and pain was shoved down, covered and ignored. *Was she not worthy of the love she was created for? She truly didn't deserve it. Was that grace even for her?*

"People's possessions end up between them and God, and, sadly, their possessions are more important to them than they should be. Those people stubbornly hang onto their ways and willfulness, refusing to submit to God. They end up sad, depressed, angry and unable to maintain good relationships. They are forever looking for something to fill the void in their souls."[1]

Submitting is on the opposite end of the spectrum to the need to be in control.

The Engineer and I watched a good movie, 'Amazing Grace'[2]

about the abolition of the slave trade in the late 1700's to early 1800's. One of my favorite quotes from the movie was, "How come you don't notice the thorns until you stop running?" There have been so many times in my life that I wasn't aware of pain, I just pushed through it.

I wasn't aware of the void in me until I was sitting quietly. Being aware of the pain. I feel miserable. I feel so desperate.

Desperate for something.

Seeking to fulfil our desperate is what some would call void filling. Only to end up desperate again! Admitting our desperate is humbling. Desperate and pride don't share the same bench.

Am I not good enough for love? Is it because I haven't allowed love to come in? Real genuine, pure, and unconditional love. Is the void, where love is supposed to go? For many years I have tried stuffing, cramming and filling that void with so many other things.

What a man desires is unfailing love. Proverbs 19:22a

My biggest little guy's feet keep growing. If you are a parent... you probably have dealt with this too! So to the shoe store we went. Well for you this might be kinda hard to imagine... but shoe stores and I have 'issues'. Not very healthy ones to say the least. So I find myself on Friday in a shoe store... we find two pairs of shoes for the biggest little guy and it just so happens that I find two pairs of shoes for the momma. Needed? Nope! Wanted and desired? Yep! Void fillers? Yep!

I won't go into all the details my friends you have a life to live out but let's just say there was OVER 24 hours of me trying to justify them. My mind and thoughts were totally consumed with those shoes! Oh and maybe there were some hours even trying, begging, pleading The Engineer to justify them or maybe this girlie was trying to have The Engineer tell me to take them back. Then he would be the bad guy.

To wrap this up...

This girl was returning those shoes on Saturday, tears, madness and frustration all went walking into that store. A whole lot of self-talk, not healthy self-talk, was going on and I am sure the lady at the return counter wondered what was going on. I am happy to report the shoes are back sitting on the shelf in the store. NOT in my closet.

My Prayer: I realize that the void, the hole, the longing of this girl's heart is to be loved. For many years I have tried and done so much to satisfy it myself. People, accomplishments, chocolate and food, shoes, relationships, ministry. Lord please forgive me for getting in the way. Purify my heart to the deepest point. I acknowledge that this is a process and it will take time. Lord help me to know that which still enslaves me. Help me to realize that the only cure is You. Help me to know my purpose is to live free in relationship with You. That nothing else will heal me, nothing else will restore me, nothing else will love me, nothing else will satisfy me but You. Lord, help me to see that nothing will fill what You designed to be filled by You- the areas of my mind, heart and soul that were created for You to fill with Your grace, love, joy, peace, contentment. I am Your creation. Submitting to that and knowing that You love me. I long to be satisfied, and I praise Your Holy name for opening my eyes this morning to it being fully in You. Amen.

Can You Hear Me Now?

A re you living in My love?

*I spoke to you again and again but you did not listen. I
called you, but you did not answer. Jeremiah 7:13*

What we want to hear and what we need to hear are not always
the same.

Before sitting down I couldn't hear with all the background noise.
When He sat me down He had my attention. Not only can I hear more
now while I sit. I am starting to listen.

I know myself and I truly struggle with seeing my humanness. I
am focused on my guilt, shame and sin. It is not pretty. So much that I
cannot see His love and grace, and if I can't see it how can I truly let it
overtake me? I know there is a point in which you go forward knowing
your heart will catch up.

*I am he, I am he who will sustain you.
I have made you and I will carry you;
I will sustain you and I will rescue you. Isaiah 46:4*

I went to be bed last night feeling so sad and overwhelmed. I still have post-surgery healing to do. So I can't really do anything. I can't lift, I can't be out running; I have to be healing. Sad about how long this is taking, sad I can't be the wife and mom I want to be. Sad that I feel bloated. Sad that I can't do 'anything'.   Lonely and sad. I wanted to wake up this morning feeling better. I am scared and feeling all alone. I HATE this. I hate that I feel weak, vulnerable, and lonely. I hate that I am not in control. I hate the thoughts that are bouncing around in my head.

It's my favorite time of day; pick the boys up from school! As I am waiting to greet them a song comes on the radio and I am reminded that God sees me, and He is with me in this.

Someday she'll understand the meaning of it all
Someday she'll trust Him and learn how to see Him
Someday He'll call her and she will come running
and fall in His arms and the tears will fall down and she'll pray,
"I want to fall in love with You."[1]

I am healing- mentally, physically, emotionally, and spiritually. I am healing.

Yesterday we visited the 'bigger' city that is about an hour from where we live. We went to a museum, ate lunch, and then we visited the mall. The Engineer took me to Victoria's Secret and handed me the debit card and informed me that he is proud of me for cleaning out my closet and that I am to go in to the store and pick out myself some 'new' stuff. He took the boys to go walk around the mall. He told me to take my time and not to rush. I had never felt more uncomfortable or out of place in my entire life. I felt as if I was walking around naked and everyone could see every single scar. As I looked around I had come to terms in my own mind that everyone else belonged in that store, but me. They deserved to be there. They fitted in there. I didn't. I didn't know what I was doing in there. The anxiety came on so fast, all I could do was get out of there. I came out of the store and felt even more anxious upon seeing The Engineer. As I had nothing to present to him! What woman in their right mind wouldn't have totally loved to have what The Engineer just gave me? I know I am messed up and need fixing. I know that God is working on me. I just wish it was being done in a hidden dark closet somewhere and no one else could see it, hear or have to deal with it. I don't even like myself right now. Impatient, judgmental, crying every second. Yuck! I hope God knows what He is doing and things can be better than this. That I can heal and be healthy.

All this seems so much. So many pieces. I am having a hard time seeing it come together. I feel so 'naked' and apart myself right now.

I am not running, as I am still healing from the surgery. So I am out for a walk and I can sense God's calming and patient presence with me. I am trying to listen. I need help hearing God's voice. I need the healing to continue in my mind, so that the thoughts rolling around in there are in control. I need the healing to continue in my soul. I need to be changed from the inside out.

My Prayer: You are calling me 'further' in this season. I know You are healing me, teaching me, correcting me, purifying me. I know You are with me. Lord I want You. Lord, help me to know this is not of my own doing. I am not going to 'get this' because my brain figures it out. It's a God thing and I need to get out of the way. Help me realize Your grace and love is NOT dependent on me. I have healing to do. I am not to ask for this 'time' to be rushed or taken from me, but rather that I am to patiently, obediently, faithfully and gracefully go through it. My heart wants to be healed. Amen.

How Will I Know?

How will I know if he really loves me?[1]

There is 'nothing' on the agenda for today. Nothing is scheduled per say while the boys are at school, well unless you count the hot tub repair guy who made it really clear on the phone yesterday that he didn't need me here! I could spend the day writing, but how do I do that? What do I write about? I feel 'pressured' that I should be doing all this writing, as if I were a writer! I guess the other thing that makes me really nervous is I have NO clue when this book is 'due'. I am not in control!

Will I ever get it right? Will I ever just have a day where I say, "Yep that one I tackled great." I feel overwhelmed in so many areas right now and I feel like I have NO control and am at a loss for what to do. Yet, at the same time there is a peace that surrounds me. Is it Love? I fear I am getting this 'wrong'. I desire to be in a closet and not out in the world. The world that I have no clue how to deal with and interact with. I can't do today.

Now I am completely at ease with not knowing all The Engineer knows, things like 'laws of physics', 'calculations', and 'arc dimensions' (he for real asked me last night for a slice of pie with a small arc dimension, seriously?) Anyway my shoe loving, creative, chocolate fan, chai drinking girlie brain does not need to know those things and really I am okay with that.

Oh and I am okay with not knowing stock exchange information too, or how meteorologists figure out how to 'guess' what weather we will be having, or how to solve the crossword puzzles in the newspapers... there are things I just don't know!

But there are things that get me in a fit. A downright icky little fit. A fit in which I am yelling out to God, "Why in the world can I not get this right? 'How come I don't know this yet?"

You know things like...

How to listen.

How to think before I speak.

How to be a calm, collected and patient momma when we are running late for school.

How to pause.

How come I just can't seem to 'know' these things?

This morning I found myself in His Word; begging God to please help me to know these things.

Guess what I found? Five little printed words that Paul penned out on a scroll many years ago that have been printed into my Bible.

I want to know Christ. Philippians 3:10

I want to know Christ.

Upon reading those words my heart shouted, "Yeah me too!!!"

Me too!

I want to know Christ. More.

I keep reading in Philippians 3 and God is speaking to my heart;

"Daughter you are Mine, and I know what you need to know. I want you to know Me, and trust Me that the rest will all workout."

My momma and I chatted on the phone this morning. We talked about knowing versus learning. What are we born knowing and what do we have to learn? Do we know love? Are we born knowing we are loved? Or do we learn that we are loved?

What life was like pre-sin in the world versus what life is like now that sin is rampant? As humans we don't know life without the presence of sin. Does this affect our belief, attitude, feelings and acceptance of love?

Adam and Eve were the only two humans to experience life pre-sin. Did they know they were loved? If they did, why would Eve risk it and taste the fruit? If she truly **knew** she was loved by God why would she need to question, doubt or risk it? Why in the world would God go through with the plan of Creation and humans knowing that sin would 'mess up' His love story? Or was this part of His plan? A relationship in which we don't assume anything and we enter in to learn who He is. We learn love. We get to experience it, the unique and personal love that He has for each one of us.

Oh, and what about those Israelites and that long journey they were on wandering around in the desert? If they knew they were loved would they have spent all that time in the desert just wandering around?

Why do we wander? Aren't we at the core just looking for love? Why would we have to look for something if we were born **knowing** it was there?

Would we try to fill voids if we **knew** we were loved?

I want to grow in the knowledge of God. Not just head knowledge, but heart knowledge, knowing that I know that I know. Yes I 'know' God loves me but that knowing currently resides in my head. I am learning to 'know' it in my heart.

I want to know His love for me has nothing to do with how I feel. So even on the foggy head wacky hormone days I know deep in my soul. Not what I 'feel' but what I know.

Allowing ourselves to 'feel' things is okay. Allowing ourselves to ask questions is also okay. To seek answers. God is aware that we are human. He created us to be human. He needs us to be human, so we can 'need' Him.

Knowing that God loves me is choosing to believe something is okay and right, even though when I look around me it doesn't appear that way. Knowing that He adores me when I don't adore myself. Knowing He loves me when I feel completely out of control mentally and emotionally.

I find myself in Song of Songs Chapter 4 and I read verse 7;
All beautiful you are, my darling; there is no flaw in you.

Oh how I long to know this, know this in my mind and heart. How I long for this to be what I live out of. In all honesty right now I find myself defending it not to be true.

Will this come to be?

Will I ever fully accept God's love for me?

The desperate need my soul has, was created for, to 'know' His love for me. The need to know in the very deepest parts of my being.

Know that I am loved by God.

Not what I 'feel' but what I know.

What if I really believed God loved me because of who He is, not because of who I am? Do you just believe? Or do you know?

How do you know?

You engage; you get involved; you go through the process. This is relationship.

Where one falls on the spectrum of beliefs is attained from information that they have been given or made aware of. To believe something is right or wrong is not always the end result, or the point to which one comes. Do we stop at believing or is the goal to know? To know because we have journeyed through the process, the process which helps us to be made aware of the right and wrong. If you tell me something is right, am I to believe you? Would you just accept it as the 'right'? I am not sure we were created to just believe. Rather to engage in a process of learning. Learning so we can know. Believing is part of that process, that which sparks our interest. I can believe something to be true, but will I ever really know it? To say I believe that the world is round, or that ice is cold, or that fire is hot, or that plane rides can be bumpy, or that coffee tastes gross (sorry to all the coffee lovers, but I just can't…) are all bold statements if I don't have something to back them up with. If I have never journeyed to see the earths curvature, or touched ice to my teeth, or stood before a fire and been hit with a spark. Or braved the back seat of a Cub with the Engineer as pilot and felt the air currents in the small little plane. Or taken a big ole swig of that steamy brown stuff most people love to drink, I just believe without really knowing.

But there are things I want to know. Things I need to know. There are beliefs that I want to know are true. Ones that must be found out in a process. I can read the Word, sing the songs, hear the sermons, attend the Bible studies; I can do and believe it all. But I am NOT changed until I know. I must know. I must know that the God of the universe, the One who fashioned me from His very hands, who created me for a purpose, loves me. Specifically loves me. So much that His Son would prove it. On a cross. All of Him proving His love for me. Not so I would just believe He loved me, but that I would learn to know.

My girlfriend Sabin leans in and speaks bold truth. "This time of sitting with God is so He can take you to the point of healing so that all you are is pure, and that your 'on purpose' is for Him about Him and is Him."

My Prayer: Thank You for being the stability in all my instability. May I know Your love, not in my head alone but in my heart, right where it was designed to fill and overflow. Thank You Lord, Amen.

Are We There Yet?

Lately I have been asking God this question, "Are we there yet?" Do you remember being in the backseat next to your sibling stuck to the hot vinyl seat in the car with no air conditioning? You were traveling somewhere that felt like a million miles away and asking that question as a little kid.

"Are we there yet?"

Or maybe now you have been on the receiving end of that question as a parent or grandparent? I have answered that question a few times in my journey of motherhood. We were blessed with a portable DVD player that enabled me to say to my little guys…

"Boys only two more Backyardigans* and we will be at Nana's house."

Most of you reading this today did not have the privilege and blessing of such a distraction on a road trip. We toughed it out… right?

"Are we there yet?"

What I am really asking;

"When will I arrive at the point where I will not struggle with pride?"

God answers:

"Daughter this is not about you arriving, achieving, earning, getting to a point or settling. This is about you knowing I love you. Don't

---

* Backyardigans are little cartoons and are usually 20 minutes in length.

add to it and don't take away from it."

For we are God's masterpiece. He has created us anew in
Christ Jesus, so we can do the good things he planned for us
long ago. Ephesians 2:10 (New Living Translation)

I realize that pride is not my original design. But to get to the masterpiece stage, I have some character building that needs to be done. Some sculpting, smoothing, and shaping must take place.

This whole sitting thing has been a ginormous struggle because of pride.

I am more concerned about what others think of me. Pride is very much woven into my flesh such as - what others think of me as a mom, wife, daughter, friend, sister, speaker, and person. For I have attached myself to this tightly. I am concerned about being embarrassed, made fun of, looking weak.

And when things rub up against my pride I just want to run. I want to fix the pain, the hurt. I want to flee the doubts, worry, and questions. I want to run.

As the pride is being exposed and taken off I am feeling icky, stinky and messy and my 'yuck' is there for everyone to see. Things don't feel all pretty right now. I am ashamed, embarrassed and still I am hanging on to my pride.

Life is being lived in the middle of the wilderness. A place that still feels very uncomfortable to me. A lot of change is going on inside this girl.

I have shouted and yelled a few times, "Why in the world do you think I can handle this?

I have wanted out of this wilderness… I have wasted some time looking for the quickest out.

Yet when I see the outs, all of them point back to Egypt and the past and there is just something, something that doesn't quite fit anymore with that place.

He led you through the great and terrible wilderness, with its fiery serpents and scorpions and thirsty ground where there was no water; He brought water for you out of the rock of flint. In the wilderness He fed you manna which your fathers did not know, that He might humble you and that He might test you, to do good for you in the end. Otherwise, you may say in your heart, 'My power and the strength of my hand made me this wealth.' But you shall remember the Lord your God, for it is He who is giving you power to make wealth, that He may confirm His covenant which He swore to your fathers, as it is this day. Deuteronomy 8:15-18 (New American Standard Bible)

Does that mean something is working out here in the wilderness?

Out here I am sensing His presence in ways that I haven't before.

I am being humbled and asked to set my pride aside.

I am thinking, *"No thank you I really don't want to be vulnerable"*… It's a pride thing.

God wants to deliver us from Egypt. He wants to bring us through the wilderness to develop our character, the very character He created us to have.

Character that cannot be developed while in Egypt or for me more personally, that couldn't be developed while I was running. I wasn't holding still long enough to hear Him. I wasn't still long enough to listen to what needed to be dealt with. Still enough to heal. Healing means the body needs to rest and be still. Still enough to repair and heal properly.

As I am tapping away on my keyboard my Ellie girl is laying on the floor next to me. Close by resting. She is content. She is in no hurry to leave my presence. She is not worried about her next meal. Her faith is strong. Knowing she is well cared for. This is where she wants to be. This moment right here. I have a lot to learn from my dog!

Now Moses was a very humble man, more humble than anyone else on the face of the earth. Numbers 12:3

To be perfectly honest I read verse 3 and think, *"Good for Moses"* - that is something I will never be. Seriously? Humble? Seeing the word humble and my name in the same sentence, really?

Moses spent 40 years in the wilderness having his character developed. He wasn't born that way.

Does that mean I will be out here for 40 years!?

God opposes the proud but gives grace to the humble. James 4:6

Could this be why for SO many years I didn't recognize love for what it was? Or why I didn't think I deserved it? Or why I didn't think I was good enough? Was I living life out of my pride and seeing things through the false security of my pride?

Tonight I am having a personal pity party. Here I am reviewing everyone else's books, and all their ministries are thriving, booming and successful. What about mine? I get in bed thinking that their names are on books, and websites, and they are being called to speak, but what about my name? As gentle and peaceful as can be God spoke to a very deep place in my heart. "Nichole I know your name and I have it written in the most important place."

See, I have tattooed your name upon my palm. Isaiah 49:16 (Living Bible)

And I know in my heart that nothing else matters. For He knows my name and He has it recorded right where it needs to be.

I wish I was her. I wish I was the girl I was created to be. The one who had faith, who didn't get sad, who had the courage to keep going. The one who didn't feel like giving up. The Jesus girl who lives somewhere inside of me. But all I can see and feel is the one who feels discouraged, tired, and selfish and 'blaw'. Will I wake up one day and not feel my feelings, the ones that feel like running? The ones inside of me that scream, *I am lonely*. Why do I struggle with the selfishness?

"Nichole I can make sense of confusion. I can order the out of order. I can, do and will make all things beautiful. In My time."

When He has tested me, I will come forth as gold. Job 23:10

This is truly my hearts' deepest desire… under all the whining, groaning and complaining. My heart desires to be pure, the purest of pure that I was created and designed to be. I know there will be a time that I will come forth.

God, pick up the pieces.
Put me back together again.
You are my praise! Jeremiah 17:14 (The Message)

My Prayer: May I not run from You. It is so easy for me to whine and complain. To see what isn't right in my eyes. I pray against the stubbornness of my heart. I pray against the desire to run and do it my way. I have rebelled I have put You to the test, please forgive me. Forgive me for testing You. Forgive me for thinking I could get out of this whole thing by pushing You away. You have brought me out, and are leading me through this wilderness. Humble me, break me, and rub off the edges that are in the way. Like only Your love can do. Amen.

How Did We Get Here?

On the eve of this New Year I am looking back at all the happenings that have unfolded over this past year, a lot has happened. I have questioned Him about this past year. I have asked Him why things had to go? Why things had to change? Why relationships struggled? How in the world He thought I could do life without estrogen and go through menopause at the age of 34? Oh and the question that piggbacks on to it… is why do The Engineer and two sweet and innocent boys have to go through this craziness? And the super big question to surpass all other questions… how in the world am I supposed to write a book?!

Trust God from the bottom of your heart; don't try to figure out everything on your own. Listen for God's voice in everything you do, everywhere you go; he's the one who will keep you on track. Don't assume that you know it all. Run to God! Run from evil! Your body will glow with health, your very bones will vibrate with life! Honor God with everything you own; give him the first and the best. Your barns will burst, your wine vats will brim over. But don't, dear friend, resent God's discipline; don't sulk under his loving correction. It's the child he loves that God corrects; a father's delight is behind all this. Proverbs 3:5-12 (The Message)

When I pause I keep hearing,
"Trust Me."

That what has happened will be purposeful for what comes to be.
Trust.
Easy for some. Hard for me.
Why?
Because I am not in control.
There is purpose in each moment. Some of which I see, much of which I don't. For those things I don't see, I will learn to trust. Because if He is saying "Trust Me," it has a purpose.
It's hard to break old habits. I want to be in control. I want to control how my body works, how I feel, who is in my life. I want to control every last detail of my life.
So here I am writing a book, and I am in control. I need to hurry up and write this book. Obedience (check). Then I can get up and go back and join the world and the life that is going on without me. Right?
Wrong! I am learning the hard way I am NOT in control. Remember I can't write. Each time I come here to my laptop all I can do is whine, complain, vent, be angry, question God and wonder, why me? Who wants to read a book that contains someone else's yuck? Seriously, how is that supposed to be motivating and encouraging? Why in the world can't I get my little act together and just do what I have been asked to do? Why can't I just sit and behave?
Is it fear? Afraid of being lonely? Afraid of missing out? Afraid of not getting it right? Afraid of what others will read?
Am I looking at this the wrong way? I definitely want **to do** something to get this whole thing progressing in the right direction. Like the direction that leads to me getting back into the action, the noise, life. I can only imagine what you, the reader is thinking at this point - it's probably the same thing as many of the people I do life with on a daily basis. The Engineer, the boys, family and friends, they are all standing by watching this all play out, which makes me want to be locked in the closet until this is all over. Or better yet, shipped off to a deserted island and sent back here when I am all 'fixed'.
I am so obsessed about this book. I have grayed the areas of this

sitting season. I am losing track of why I have been sat down.

"Seek My face Nichole. Seek Me. Lift up your eyes to Me. Lift up your heart to Me. Lift up your hands to Me- so that I may come in. I want to fill you up. I want to consume your thoughts. I want to rule and take over your life fully. Do you believe My Word? Do you trust My love?"

How did we get here?

This year has been a journey. A journey that I did NOT think I could endure. Stops that lasted too long for me. Visits that I was not mature enough to make. Times that I just knew my heart would break.

How did we get here?

I don't know. I don't know how I am sitting at His precious feet right now in this moment.

Some might call it religion. Not me.

Some might call it obedience. Not me.

No rather my heart is whispering, "Nichole it's grace and love. You don't have to know to understand it, just live in it My daughter."

How did we get here?

His love has brought me into this location.

Sitting with God in these past few months has overwhelmed me in many ways. I don't ever want to be running so far ahead that I can't hear and sense His heartbeat, feel His hand upon me, or hear His voice.

I just came in from cleaning up the yard. It's such a beautiful spring day. High 70's, blue sky, slight breeze. The sunlight and warmth feel so good. As I worked I realized where I was in life. Stronger. I have spent part of yesterday and this morning realizing what I have is all I need. Above that is want and greed. I am **'sitting contently'**. Actively. In the present sense. Do I have this perfected? No way. Each day brings awareness of new things/situations/areas of fine-tuning. As I worked out in the yard I realized how I want things quickly, instantly. I want the yard to be so clean, every weed pulled, every pinecone picked up, and the grass perfectly level and green. Just like my life, every detail in place. For years I worked and strived to try and achieve just that. But here I sit with all of my flaws and areas that need fine-tuning and somehow I am at peace. Knowing I don't have everything figured out.

My location, my height, my blood pressure, and my perspective are all changing.

I am trying to allow His peace and calmness to surround me.

The sitting has become easier. I am truly learning so much. This time is preparation for what is next.

God, teach me lessons for living so I can stay the course. Give me insight so I can do what you tell me — my whole life one long, obedient response. Guide me down the road of your commandments; I love traveling this freeway! Give me a bent for your words of wisdom, and not for piling up loot. Divert my eyes from toys and trinkets, invigorate me on the pilgrim way. Affirm your promises to me — promises made to all who fear you. Deflect the harsh words of my critics — but what you say is always so good. See how hungry I am for your counsel; preserve my life through your righteous ways! Psalm 119:33-40 (The Message)

As the days go on I can sense that my balance has been off.

I was choosing to strive over serve.

I was trying to make things happen instead of joining Him.

I was avoiding instead of obeying.

Not healing is truly staying captive and remaining in Egypt.

Taking steps to healing is walking towards the One. It's not the speed at which you are traveling, but the direction.

Something is changing for me.

A whole new focus, smell and place of being.

For I find myself not somewhere I would have taken myself, but truly enjoying being here.

These are the important things: The moment, in which my girl dog lays at my side, faithfully, resting, giving companionship. The moment that holds green tea from Chinatown in San Francisco in the black coffee mug that sits to the right of my monitor. My feet that are socked in bright pink socks. Socks that were worn with tennis shoes so I could ride along on my bike with the boys to school. The dryer that tumbles the clean load of whites in such a rhythmic pattern. The laptop fan that comes on to keep it cool. All in a home that isn't about size, floor plan, but all about a place to gather as Team Hamblin. To regroup, to share, to fill our minds, bodies and souls with nourishment.

Being here in this moment. Not overly concerned how I got here, but rather being present in this moment.

My Prayer: I pray for You to flood my mind and heart, and remind me it's not where this is taking me, or what's happening next, or where I need to be going, but that I am with You. You! It's about being with You, hearing from You, listening to You, applying what You are telling me, living in relationship with You. I pray Father God for a strong focus on what truly matters. A renewal of what You have called me to. Being in relationship with You. I praise You for the release and freedom from striving, knowing You are in control is such a peaceful freeing place to live, I desire to stay here and yet know in my humanness that I will try and get back… so help me to stay tight to the reality of this peace, You! Amen.

PART 2:

Stand

Now Stand

Have you ever felt awkward? You know a little uncomfortable? Or maybe a lot of uncomfortable?

I'm picturing the scene from 'Bambi' when Bambi is trying to stand up on the ice.

Bambi is trying something new- to stand and walk on the ice. It feels awkward, difficult and uncomfortable. Maybe even some anxiety is pulsating through.

So I stand here with my knees all wobbly. Anxious.

Part of me would rather just stay sitting; it has become comfortable. Safe. Funny, that over a year ago I was way awkward, anxious and uncomfortable in this position. I have gotten used to sitting. And I think that is part of what makes it time to adjust.

It's a change of posture - from sitting to standing.

I am staring at the file opened on my laptop labeled 'the book', the one I have no stinkin' clue how to write. The hugeness of this feels tangible right now. The weight of it is on my shoulders. All I really want to do is crawl up on my bed and take a nap. Where to begin? What to say? I have a heart and mind full of questions I am yelling out. Why in the world did He pick the girl who really doesn't even understand sentence structuring? The girl who forgets to proofread her Facebook status? Editing and I tend to hangout in different circles of friends. I am pre-apologizing to my editor. So sorry!

There are a whole lotta girls out there right now writing and they are doing a fantastic job. They are on the bestseller's lists, and on the front shelves when you walk in the bookstores. They most likely sat in the front of the class in English and paid attention. I think the only thing I happened to pay attention to in English class was if everyone's shoes went with their outfits.

I am scared beyond belief, scared that I won't 'do it right'.

Tyler asked me the other night about getting the book published and I wanted to run out of the room, I felt sick to my stomach! Oh son that is a whole 'nother worry for your momma. Then the amazing calm and collected Engineer chimed in, "Tyler, mommy wasn't asked to go there, she was just asked to write the book."

I am reminded that I am not standing alone. He will be with me. He knows all my fears, worries, and doubts, and He still asked me to do this.

A huge investment from Him to me was made this past year. My heart, mind and soul were attentive.

I stand in awe of the investment He has made, not just this past year, but in the total 34 years He has lovingly held my hand and walked with me.

I stand next to a man who I was created for, The Engineer. A man who needs a passionate encourager to stand next to him.

I stand to cheer on two boys, The T-Squad, who have great purpose and many years ahead of them to live life for their Jesus.

I stand in reverence of a God who has done great things, and will continue.

I stand in amazement of a season that I learned so much and I let go of so much.

I stand more healed from where I was a year ago. I stand knowing I was supposed to sit.

Remember the song *Stand*[1] by R.E.M.; the lyrics of the song ask us to think about where we are. Where we are standing.

So I stand here.

I am celebrating standing. You would too if you had been sitting so long. Maybe I am a little quick to celebrate. Maybe I don't realize I am entering another unknown.

So I stand. In His strength. I will move when He moves me. I will go where He takes me, knowing fully well I stand because of Him. I can stand now because I learned how to sit.

This morning I am reading 2 Peter 1:12-21. Peter is encouraging us to remain in Him and to continue growing. To stand on the firm foundation of who He is, and to build from there. I am learning to thank Him for this point in my life, a time in which He so lovingly and graciously knocked down a prideful and selfish foundation I built for myself.

Love breaks us of our pride.

I thank Him for calling my name loud, getting my attention. I am grateful to Him for sitting me down.

My soul clings to You; Your right hand upholds me.
Psalm 63:8 (New American Standard Bible)

My Prayer: Lord I pray I continue to listen. I desire a heart that stays humble and teachable. Thank You for Peter's example of being in tune with You, Your way and Your Word. I thank You for reminding me today that Your Word is perfect, holy and pure. That Your Word was written just how You wanted it. You, the power of Your Holy Spirit worked through the lives of Your people to share Your heart. May I know that Your Word is for me, to read, hear, to truly hear and apply it each and every day. Amen.

The Way That I Am

I have this vision of myself. I am standing in a perfectly white dress, my hair is all done pretty, and new shoes are on my feet. I am presenting myself this way to cover up the need I have on the inside. The outside presentation is to hide the imperfections on the inside. Hide the void. I feel I am lacking. I am standing in a line waiting to approach my Creator. How can I come before God lacking and needing? Wanting? I have a bunch of 'yuck' that needs to be dealt with. I hide behind a 'done up' appearance. Over the years I would shove all the 'yuck' down and hide it. I didn't want others to see this, and honestly I didn't want to see it either. So I am standing in this line. I'm broken, desperate and in need of a Healer. As I wait I am anxious, nervous, and internally asking, *'Am I good enough; did I get everything right; will I be enough?'* I allow others to go before me; I am not ready. I stand in line. Those ahead of me in the line are given grace; they are pardoned. They receive love. As I watch the line move He doesn't turn anyone away, and yet I believe He is going to turn me away.

I stand in line with a beautifully wrapped box in my hands. The line moves closer to the front. It's almost my turn.

Before me is my Creator, on His Throne. I present the wrapped box to Him. The box contains all my brokenness, hurt, mistakes, and failures. I have cleaned them all up and go to hand them over. I see my Creator look down upon me and in a voice that sounds all knowing, I hear Him say, "Sorry daughter but there is just not enough grace to cover over all of that."

I am not accepted. I am not good enough. So I turn and leave, still broken and unhealed. I walk away from His presence and to the back of the line I go. Maybe next time I will have it right. Maybe next time!

Really I never want to approach this again. I am back to running. I know how to do it. It seems so much easier to keep running and doing. 'On the go' means I don't have time to heal. Truly heal. The running helps distract. The pain is not as noticeable. God feels even more distant. I wasn't worthy. I would have to try harder or just come to accept this was as good as it gets for me.

Getting it right is something I so badly want in my life. For I thrive on it. Truly living the right life. The prideful, perfectionistic, controlling personality needs others to see that I have my act together. This getting it right spills over into all areas of my life. I want to get it right as a wife, a daughter, and a friend and especially as a mom.

Who will love me for me?
Not for what I have done.
Or what I will become.
Who will love me for me?[1]

Can I be loved just the way that I am?

Yet you refuse to come to Me to have life. John 5:40

My Prayer: I am praying that the simplicity of this verse reaches into my heart today. I can sit here and think of many hours, days, weeks, months and years that my pride and selfishness have kept me from coming to You Lord. Thinking I had to be better. Or I had to get my act together first. Or thinking I just wasn't good enough - why come? That Your love and grace wasn't 'enough' to fix and heal me. Thank You for Your patience with me. I thank You that I am learning to allow Your love to cover me, to surround me and to go before me. Amen.

Realization of who I Created God to Be

It's early fall, boys are back in school, and I as the momma, have some learning to do too. Each season of parenting brings new challenges. I am sitting in my comfy chair all wrapped snug in a blanket reading a book that was shared with me on how to parent. I am expecting to get parenting skills and instead I am met with a very scary realization;

I have created my own image of God.

What? Am I hearing this right?

I have created my own image of God. I have built Him up in my mind with false characteristics. With a personality He doesn't have. How did this happen? Why did this happen? When did this happen?

You are always on their lips but far from their hearts. Jeremiah 12:2b

This verse describes my living conditions for too many years of my life. I knew how to talk about Him, but I didn't truly know Him. I had created an image of God as a dictator, one who was very controlling and judgmental. One who was not accepting or forgiving. I was doing all the talking. I was not listening or hearing.

How I see God, frames how I see everything. Now this is a 'duh' moment, but truly a deep moment for me. For in my pride and the need to control I have created God to be;

- Judgmental - His first reaction to everything I think, say and do is to judge me. To point out all the mistakes and flaws.
- Incomplete - not enough for me.
- Withholding of forgiveness until I have achieved or earned it.

Do I believe that God is disappointed in me? Did God create me how He wants me to be? Was I created in His image with unique characteristics that are needed to fulfill the purpose He has willed my life to have? Do I believe God loves me? Not dependent on who I am or what I have done. Do I know God is love? Do I believe that I don't have to qualify for His love? Can God be added to or taken from? Can I make His love for me possible or not possible? Will I choose to acknowledge His love for me?

As I type this out for you to read, I am embarrassed. How did this happen? I so badly want my story right now to be that I am a victim and that this is someone else's fault. I am sure the words would type out so much faster on the screen. Rather my fingers pause with each word and struggle to complete these sentences. As I type these words there is a release of pride. Light is shining onto what has been in the dark - in the dark for so long. This is hard to share, because I am not the victim of anyone else's mistakes but my own. They are my choices, my decisions, and my false belief system of thinking that I could do it myself. My pride, stubbornness, and control issues are all from me.

I am broken.

In my messy sin I created God's characteristics.

My created image of God.

They were my thoughts/opinions/views on how God was, is and would be. What He would say or do. I created His response, and thus created Him - my vision of Him turning His head when I approached Him because He was disgusted with me. I held onto this vision for so long.

*With whom, then, will you compare God? To what
image will you liken him? Isaiah 40:18*

He is not man made and more specifically not Nichole made! His love
is not to be dictated, controlled, managed or arranged by me.

But to hear what You would say
Word of God speak
Washing my eyes to see
To be still and know[1]

I am here to write. I am easily tempted to write what you would want
to read. Especially when I hear Tyler ask last night during prayer circle,
"Mom can I read your book when you're done?" The girl who is trans-
formed in her Jesus, shouts, "Yes of course!"

This morning as I sit here at this keyboard I think of all the thoughts,
words and actions I would not want my eight year old son to know. The
'stuff' that would taint the picture of his momma! I fear this could over-
ride what Jesus has done in my life. Then I pause. Nothing I have said or
will say will diminish Him in any way. I am not capable of such a thing.
If I am not willing to share my heart then I am not willing to allow God
to do what He needs to do. For really I am not the key component to this
process. Not at all.

My Prayer: Lord I know what it's like to be bound so tightly in pride
and stubbornness. To push against You out of fear. Fear that I was not
good enough for You. Fear that You couldn't possibly love me. Help
me to truly see this for what it is. Pride is thinking that I am in control
of You, and I am NOT. I cannot control Your feelings for me. Father,
forgive me for the choices, and decisions I made. I pray Lord for the
awareness that only You can bring to me and my life. To see things in
Your light and move forward in them. To trust that when You say it,
You mean it. You are faithful, righteous, pure, Holy, honest, forgiving,

loving, and trustworthy. May I truly get who You are Lord. I want to know You. I want to experience life with You. May my thoughts, words, and actions come under Your authority. Amen.

The Heart of the Matter

I don't want to introduce you to this whole idea. Mainly because I don't want to credit him with anything or even admit I fell for his nastiness. But as I think back over the years, there is definitely an enemy of my soul. He is a definite killjoy who wants to see me broken, destroyed, and running from my Creator. Why?

The heart is hopelessly dark and deceitful,
a puzzle that no one can figure out.
But I, God, search the heart
and examine the mind.
I get to the heart of the human.
I get to the root of things.
I treat them as they really are,
not as they pretend to be. Jeremiah 17:9-10 (The Message)

We are more alike than you and I realize. Something all humans have in common - sin. My sin and brokenness might be a different color and texture than yours but it's still sin. Sin that separates me from my Creator. Separated! There are not depths or levels to sin. There is no sin that makes us too far gone. For the reach of the Creator can far outreach the distance in which we have taken ourselves. When we allow this truth to come and meet us right where we are, the sin doesn't seem so binding. So overwhelming. Love comes and shines a different perspective. God's perspective of sin is way different than ours. It's not in our lives so that He can remove it and administer punishment. What if it was there so that He could remove it because He loves us? What if His allowance of our free will, our choices were so that the depth and sincerity of His pure love could be proven? *I want to know His love is real.* I want to know that His love isn't something I just hear about, or read about. I want and need to know in the deepest depths of my heart, mind and soul that His love is for me. Then it will change how I see and do life.

The enemy wants to keep me bound up in the dark, chained up in fear. His real fight is not against me, but rather against my Creator. The enemy uses me in his nasty game. Sin! Sin is what keeps us from knowing our Creator. Knowing Love. The enemy has many tactics to keep us from knowing who we really are. He feeds us lies, he entertains us with the ways of this world, he supports our harmful addictions of pride, and the need to control.

I read Chapter 4 of the book of John and I am reminded I am not alone in sin. Jesus seeks out a woman at a well. Jesus was a Jew and she, was a Samaritan woman. At this point in time men were not allowed to be talking with women in public, let alone a Samaritan woman. The Jews did not associate with the Samaritans. Jesus initiates a conversation with her. She has no clue who this man is. Yet she is very familiar with who she is. A woman enslaved to sin. During the conversation with this woman Jesus reveals more of Himself to her by calling her in her sin, and He shows her she has a NEED for Him. Jesus doesn't call out her sin to bring her shame or embarrass her. He does it to show her the void she has been trying to fill with love and romantic relationships. He is showing her that she has been trying to fill her loneliness with worldly desires.

The diagnosis of sin – well it's enough to take me from this current position of standing and knock me down and out. Sin is ugly. Gross. Disgusting. It is not something I want to admit to. But it's in me. It's there. And it's the inflow. I am not able to breathe in deeply enough. I am not able to think clearly enough. Sin!

For a man is a slave to whatever has mastered him. 2 Peter 2:19

Nichole is a slave to whatever has mastered her.

We are all born as slaves, slaves to sin. We are a slave to whatever controls us. What is controlling me? What has a dominating influence over me? My *slavery* looks like this: I have to be in complete control of everything; I have pride issues; and when I get stressed about something I tend to eat over the feelings of stress. (Now it's hard not to want to backspace that!).

I can think of so many things that have mastered me in my life.

Pride. Selfishness. People's approval. Money. Food. Shopping.

Am I truly living my life as a free person or if I am still stuck in the slave mentality?

It is for freedom that Christ has set us free. Stand firm, then, and do not let yourselves be burdened again by a yoke of slavery. Galatians 5: 1

As I was driving in the car today, I heard God's sweet and yet all-powerful voice reminding me, "Nichole I paid a very high price for your life and your freedom, don't you think you can trust me? Nichole I want you to be free and live like you're free. Living like you are free, means you will put all your trust and faith in me."

Freedom[2] – 'The right to enjoy all the privileges or special rights of citizenship, membership'

If I am hauling around my *yoke of slavery*, how can I be living like I am free? I am stuck in a slave mentality.

My Prayer: My pride keeps me from You. That is sin. Sin keeps me from You. Thank You for getting to the heart of the matter. For not giving up on me. For truly healing and restoring me. Thank You for this continued process. Jesus, You bring grace and love to the deepest parts. Thank You for loving me daily. Amen.

Arms Wide Open

I remember standing in that line during PE class waiting to have my name called for teams. I absolutely hated that line; I wasn't so athletic, which meant I was not one of the first ones to be chosen. So towards the end I am standing there among the 'not so good enough's' wishing very badly that PE was not a requirement of high school graduation. This was back when I truly thought that the 'real world' was high school and that it was the center of the universe.

You did not choose me, but I chose you. John 15:16a

I have been chosen. Here I am standing. Listening. Paying attention.

This is deeper than the time that I accepted Jesus as my Savior when I was thirteen years old.

There is something I need to see with a new perspective. He's led me here.

To the cross.

Many had died on a cross. Punishment for what they had done. But this man had done no wrong.

His arms are wide open. He wants me to know this was not just for everyone else. It was for me too.

For the Son of Man came to seek and to save what was lost. Luke 19:10

Life is messy, yucky, difficult, hard, and not much fun at times. So was the cross. And yet in every detail it was perfect, perfect love.

This is love; not that we loved God, but that He loved us and sent His Son as an atoning sacrifice for our sins. 1 John 4:10

Everything He endured, put up with, and took, it was all for me. So I wouldn't have to go through it. He chose to do it for me. All the sin He took upon Himself - everything that kept me from knowing Him fully. All that created that dark empty void. He took on the world, its filth, its persecution, its slander and its ugliness it was the ultimate burden. He chose to hang on a cross.

He showed them the full extent of His love. John 13:1

Love chose the cross.
Love carried the cross up the hill.
Love got on that cross.
Love never took His eyes off His Father.
Love knew that the cross would bring fulfilment to every void.
Love declared on a public cross that death and sin could rule no more. No more.

'It is finished.' John 19:30

Finished. Completed. Done.
Sin was done. Separation was done.
That the dark void that separates God from His people was filled. Filled with the life giver Jesus.
I need to hear what 'is done' in my life. I need to know my past, my sin, my old life… *it is finished.*

*For He has rescued us from the dominion of darkness and
brought us into the kingdom of the Son he loves, in whom we have
redemption, the forgiveness of sins. Colossians 1:13-14*

For years I was focused on rules. The Law. Following the list of Do's
and Don'ts.

I am reminded why Jesus came. Love left heaven above. Love came
to earth to live life with us and to ultimately make that a reality for
eternity.

*For Christ died for sins once for all, the righteous for the
unrighteous, to bring you to God. 1 Peter 3:18*

I had been living in the confidence of myself. Thinking my good
works could try and earn my salvation. That is disrespectful to the cross.

Jesus doesn't need my performances. **He needs my heart!**

Accepting my free gift of salvation at the age of thirteen was just
the beginning!

I came to God fearful of His judgment of me. I came to represent
myself. It was all me. My deeds, my sin, my tap dancing, my trying, all
wrapped up in my pride. I thought I was in control. I was trying to carry a cross. I was denying the love act of Jesus. My Savior who died for
me, so that, I could approach God with no shame, no sin, no pride, no
need to be in control. I could stand before God with nothing because
my Jesus gave everything.

*But because of His great love for us, God, who is rich in mercy,
made us alive in Christ even when we were dead in transgressions
- it is by grace you have been saved. Ephesians 2:4-5*

'That her sin has been paid for' Isaiah 40:2

Because of the cross I can come into a love and grace filled relationship with Jesus. One that not only saves us from sin, but gives us life abundant.

I have swept away your sins like a cloud.
I have scattered your offenses like the morning mist.
Oh, return to me, for I have paid the price to set you free.
Isaiah 44:22 (New Living Translation)

My Prayer: Thank You Lord for seeking me and saving me. May I accept salvation for me. Please forgive me for void filling with the things of this world. Forgive me for running all these years from You, and not allowing You to heal me. Lord forgive me for the guilt, pain, anger, frustration, worry, and all other 'baggage, junk and stuff' I have carried over the years associated with this. Thank You Lord for forgiving me. I believe You have. I pray now that I can be purposeful about forgiving myself. Going on in You. I know the enemy does NOT want this to be. So Lord, guard my mind and heart right now and throughout this continued journey. That I will truly know Your love for me, a love that You declared publicly on a cross. That is a love that I will never fully understand, but one that I truly desire to live in. I desire to live guilt free, and worry free. I desire to live fully in the peace You have left for me. Your grace still amazes me, truly, that for me You died. Lord may each moment be filled with You and may my awareness of just who You are continue to grow, into a deep and intimate heart knowledge. Amen.

You Are God Alone

I was being made aware that in my humanness I had created a false image of God. One that was judgmental, strict, and harsh. I created Him to be a God who was focused more on rule following than relationship.

I had not been seeing God clearly.

I was hungry for the truth. The truth of the Real God. Not my created version. Not who the world told me He was. Not who the church, or the pastor, or a song on the radio. I wanted, *I needed* to know who God really was.

I keep asking that the God of our Lord Jesus Christ, the glorious Father, may give you the Spirit of wisdom and revelation, so that you may know Him better. I pray also that the eyes of your heart may be enlightened in order that you may know the hope to which He has called you, the riches of His glorious inheritance in the saints, and His incomparably great power for us who believe. The power is like the working of His mighty strength. Ephesians 1:17-19

I need to know God.

I go to the source. The Word. The Truth. The Life. The Bible.

Where God has written to me about Himself and His great love for me.

I am hearing there is a difference in knowing God mentally and knowing Him spiritually. One will change me from the inside out.

I am reading about the characteristics of God. What makes Him, who He is?

- He has always been. There is no beginning and no end to Him. He has existed forever and forever He will be. He is **eternal**. (Exodus 3:14).

- God does not owe His being to any other. He is **self-existent**. (Exodus 3:14 The Message, Psalm 90:2, Colossians 1:15-17).

- He has no limit. For He goes beyond the ordinary limits. He is **superior**. (Isaiah 55:8-9 The Message, Isaiah 57:15, Psalm 113:5-6 The Message, John 8:23).

- God is not absent or distant. He is present everywhere at the same time. He is **everywhere**. (Jeremiah 23:23-34).

- He is unlimited in knowledge. He understands all. He is **all knowing**. (Psalm 147:5, Romans 11:33 The Message, 1 John 3:20).

- God is in control. He holds all authority and power. He is **sovereign**. (Ephesians 1:11 The Message).

- There is no end to His unlimited power. He is **all-powerful**. (Jeremiah 32:17, Matthew 19:26, Romans 11:36).

- God is constant, stable, fixed. He is **unchanging**. (Malachi 3:6, James 1:17).

- His authority displays His honest and fair nature. He is **just**. (Psalm 99:4 The Message).

- God is good, moral, and honest. He is **righteous**. (Psalm 19:7-9, Psalm 145:17 The Message).

- He is kind. God is generous. He is **good**. (Psalm 25:8, Psalm 100:5).

- God is pure. He is **holy**. (1 Peter 1:16, Revelation 4:8).

- We receive mercy and pardon from God. He is **grace**. (Romans 3:24, Romans 5:20, 21 The Message, Hebrews 4:16 The Message).

- God is present and actively participating with His creation. He is **indwelling**. (Haggai 2:5, Acts 17:27-28).

- He is quick to forgive. God is compassionate. He is **mercy**. (Hebrews 4:16, Ephesians 2:4 The Message, Titus 3:5).

- He is fond of us. He is fully devoted to us. He is passionate about us. God is **love**. (Deuteronomy 7:7-8, Romans 5:8, Romans 8:35, 39, 1 John 4:8, 16).

That is a pretty impressive attribute list. Our Creator is amazing. And I stand in awe as I read that.

And I stand, I stand in awe of You
And I stand, I stand in awe of You
Holy God to whom all praise is due
I stand in awe of You[1]

I can take this in as head knowledge but for this to become heart knowledge I believe God will have me experience these different characteristics about Himself in intimate and personal ways.

"It is theology not of the head but of the heart."[2]

If I had to pick a favorite trait about God it would be;

God is love. 1 John 4:8

Love.
This is it. For years I have wanted to know, truly know that I was loved. Loved in spite of who I was, the mistakes I had made or would

still make. Truly, purely and unconditionally loved.

So just maybe The Beatles were right; *'All you need is love'*.

They say, (they being the wise ones who have lived longer and learned life's lessons), that hindsight is 20/20. It's obvious now looking back to see what the huge void in my life was. What I desired more than anything. What I spent so many years trying to earn, strive for, be good enough for. Love. I wanted to be loved. I wanted to feel loved. Not knowing any better I thought love was something you had to earn and deserve and be good enough for. I believed it for so long it became my truth, my belief my reality. I can remember trying to earn, strive for and be good enough for anyone's love. And if I wasn't then love would not be there. And in doing so I found ways to make myself 'feel' loved, not realizing it was a false love. A false love that never filled the void. I was left wanting. Still needing.

Needing love.

Let your face shine on your servant; save me in your unfailing love.
Psalm 31:16

I now realize I need this love.

My Prayer: You have always been and will always be. You are forever and unchanging. You are God alone and have complete control. You have no limit or boundary. You are all knowing and powerful. You are generous, fair, forgiving and righteous. You are Love. Thank You God for being always present. May the knowledge of who You are move from my head to my heart. Amen.

What Love is This?

Ihave been guilty of using the love of another to fill the void and ache in me. It proved out to not be the right fit. This is not the fault of the other person but rather me seeking the wrong source. I have also been known to ask shoes to fill the void. The more shoes I purchased the more I would drown out the ache of the void. I am not happy to admit, but food, especially a 9x13 pan of chocolate brownies, has also been asked to take away the lonely, desperate and needing feelings that the void so loudly shouts. Everything that I have tried humanly to fill the void has never been successful.

> *I wanna know what love is*
> *I want you to show me*
> *I wanna feel what love is*
> *I know you can show me.*[1]

So what fills the void, the ache?

Could it be love?

But don't we live in a world surrounded with love? Love that is so quick to appear?

Is it true love? Genuine and pure love?

What makes God's love different from that of the world's love?

WHAT LOVE IS THIS?

What love is this that you gave your life for me
And made a way for me to know you.[2]

- Love was selfless and made a sacrifice. Love came to help. Love endured the cross.
- Love came to heal. Love came to provide a better way of life.
- Love that has no boundaries. Love that will go over and beyond.
- Love that always endures and never gives up. Love that is patient and sincere.
- Love that doesn't see through human eyes on human terms.
- Love that sees the heart and original design of each one created in His likeness.
- Love protects and defends. Love holds out against the enemy.
- Love sustains and is not impaired by human free will.
- Love doesn't turn away from the hard and difficult to love.
- Love is patient and tolerable.
- Love supports and strengthens against adverse force or influence of any kind.
- Love endures forever.

We're all like sheep who've wandered off and gotten lost.
We've all done our own thing, gone our own way.
And God has piled all our sins, everything we've done wrong,
on him, on him. Isaiah 53:6 (The Message)

I am a sheep who sometimes gets herself out of the pin and lost. The Great Shepherd comes and finds me and brings me back.

For the Son of Man came to seek and to save what was lost. Luke 19:10

He pursues me. He rescues me.

And when he finds it, he joyfully puts it on his shoulders Luke 15:5

His reaction towards me is completely full of extraordinary love.

A shepherd going after His lost sheep. As I read about this one lost sheep, I am sensing that in my human nature and tendency to run I can get off course very easily and get myself lost. God has come out to find me. He finds me, places me on His shoulders joyfully and carries me back home. Why would He do this for me? And do it joyfully? I know my humanness. It is not pretty looking. Am I focused on my guilt, shame and sin? So much that I cannot see His love and grace? Is there a point in which you go knowing your heart will catch up?

What love is this?

A love that will go down deep to reach below all that yuck I have in me and root it out.

"Nichole I love You. I want you Nichole to get that, to understand that, to fully wrap yourself in that."

That's when God broke me. For love doesn't let us settle. Love doesn't make us work harder. Pure love captures us, causes us to sit, allows us to heal, and is patient enough to go with us. Long enough to heal; truly heal. I ask Him to keep speaking. I desire to listen. But **more** than listen, I desire for this love to pour down on me. To over-take me. To change me. This Love will be right. For this Love will change me. A love that will capture my heart. This Love will heal the soul. This love will lead to a relationship. A love that I will never fully understand.

As I am getting ready this morning a song is playing on the radio and I hear these words, *'I write about love because I want it so much'.*[3] My all-consuming thoughts and my heart's deepest need. What we need we seek! I have spent so much time and energy seeking it. Time spent trying to fill the need with other things. Anything that makes the 'feel-ings' of loneliness and emptiness go away.

This morning as the T-Squad and I are eating breakfast, Tyler explains to me the difference between permanent and temporary tattoos. "Mom you know that temporary tattoos and permanent tattoos are exactly the same. Except that temporary tattoos don't last forever and permanent ones do!" I just love the perspective of my young little guy. All the earthly things we try will be temporary. Only God's love is permanent.

No, in all these things we are more than conquerors through Him who loved us. For I am convinced that neither death nor life, neither angels nor demons, neither the present nor the future, nor any powers, neither height nor depth, nor anything else in all creation, will be able to separate us from the love of God that is in Christ Jesus our Lord." Romans 8:37-39

Not only is love a permanent thing, it also never fails.

Love never fails. 1 Corinthians 13:8

Love is enduring.

Give thanks to the LORD, for he is good; his love endures forever. 1 Chronicles 16:34

Love is patient.

He is patient with you. 2 Peter 3:9

My Prayer: Thank You Lord for seeking me and saving me. To show me love. A love that feels different. A love that is all consuming. For no matter what the world has going on, I am starting to feel peace. A love that had been there all along. Love that makes me want to breathe it in deeper. I will never fully comprehend love like that, but Lord I am tired of trying to earn it, understand it, achieve it, explain it, and grasp it. A Love that is not containable or explainable. I know I want it, need it and was created for it! I don't deserve it, can't and won't ever earn it. I just need to accept it. I am in awe of Your love for me. I pray that I allow You to continue to saturate me in Your love. Thank You Lord for Your amazing patience with me. Amen.

Enough

There was so much wrong with the vision I had standing before God. I had an unhealthy perspective. I had created God from my perspective. I had created God out of my human brokenness. The God I created was harsh, cold, judgmental, non-accepting, and hard to please. I was a girl who created God because she had to be in control. But He isn't man made; He can't be controlled, or dictated to.

I thought I had to have all of it taken care of before I even came into His presence. I had things all backwards. I thought what mattered most was the presentation - how things appeared on the outside. I thought I could even present my sin in such a way that would be 'better' so I would be able to have His love and grace. Upon learning that I had created God I was devastated. Devastated and embarrassed that I had believed this lie. This lie that the enemy kept me tightly bound and had kept me from truly seeing the real God. It kept me from seeing and knowing Love.

> *Put off your old self… to be made new in the attitude of*
> *your minds; and put on the new self, created to be like God in*
> *true righteousness and holiness. Ephesians 4:22-24*

I am standing in line. I am barefoot. My hair is loosely curled and waving in the breeze. My dress is not perfectly clean. My hands are empty.

*In Him and through faith in Him we may approach God
with freedom and confidence. Ephesians 3:12*

In the old vision I was standing in the line with my gift in my hands and waiting to see if whether God will accept me or not. I realize now I was coming in my own strength, I was coming on my own… I wasn't coming in God. I wasn't coming in His love and grace.

*Let us then approach the throne of grace with confidence, so that we may
receive mercy and find grace to help us in our time of need Hebrews 4:16*

I come before my Creator.

I see The One True God, my Creator; the One who has His arms wide open and is ready to embrace me.

I am standing before Him, there are tears running down my face, my feet are bare, and there is no gift in my hands. I get to the front of the line; I am standing there. God is reaching out His arms and He pulls me in. "That's my girl! I love you Nichole."

*Oh, may I then in Him be found;
Dressed in His righteousness alone,
Faultless stand before the throne.[1]*

For He is a place of love, safety and refuge.

*This is what the Lord says, 'fear not for I have redeemed you; I have summoned you by
name, you are mine; I give Egypt your ransom; Since you are precious and honored in my
sight, and because I love you; everyone who is called by my name, whom I created for my
glory, whom I formed and made'; Forget the former things; do not dwell on the past. See, I
am doing a new thing! The people I formed for myself that they may proclaim my praise.
(Isaiah 43 paraphrased)
Being confident of this, that He who began a good work in you will carry it on to
completion until the day of Christ Jesus. Philippians 1:6*

Confident, that's a word with a whole lot of weight. I need to be standing to be able to plant my little feet sclidly on that confidence.

I keep reading that it's Him who is doing all the work.

He started it in me. Sometimes I think because of my stubborn thickness it takes a lot more 'tools and time' with me. He's doing the work. And He is going to complete the job. He's not going to just 'try' or give it His best shot, and He won't get tirec. He is going to complete it.

I wanna tell you something
You're more important than you'll ever know
Do you know that you're loved?[2]

I couldn't have imagined myself here.

Where is here?

It's a place where I feel heaven reaching down. Reaching down to touch the heart of a girl.

A girl who doesn't deserve the reach or the effort.

A girl who can't wrap her head around the why of the reach.

A girl who can't breathe it in fast enough.

This moment holds more than I can process. And that is why it has to be His thing.

A divine moment!

He isn't up there rushing me through this one. He waits patiently.

This moment matters.

As tears continue to flow, I'm taking a deep breath, and I am choosing not to try and 'figure' this out.

This is not something to be figured out, but rather to allow it to happen.

Grace.

Love.

Redemption.

Healing.

Not my way, but His.

To allow Love to come and do His thing.

Living on purpose means I live out what God says about me.
- God says I am loved. (2 Thessalonians 2:16)
- God says I am saved by grace. (Ephesians 2:5, 8)
- God says He knows all about me. (Psalm 139)
- God says I am blessed. (Philippians 4:19)
- God says I am His daughter. (2 Corinthians 6:18, Galatians 3:26)
- God says He created me in His image. (Genesis 1:27)
- God says He has a plan and purpose for my life. (Romans 8:28)
- God says He will provide for me. (Matthew 6:25-26, Philippians 4:19)
- God says He will protect me. (Psalm 138:7, 2 Corinthians 4:8-9)
- God says He will never leave me. (Deuteronomy 31:6, Hebrews 13:5)
- God says He will give me the power to overcome and be victorious. (1 Corinthians 15:57)

In this journey I am coming to realize it has **NOTHING** to do with my church attendance, how often I read my Bible, if I get all the words right to my prayers. It isn't about who I am at all. He loves me because of who He is. Not because of who I am. He loves me because He created me. He loves me because He sees me through His son, Jesus. He loves me because I am His daughter. Not because of something I figured out, earned, or even strived to become. I didn't 'become' any-thing. He created me to be His daughter. I am enough. He loves me.

95

My Prayer: It feels like it has taken a lot for a girl like me to know she is loved by a God like You. I feel like I have grown so much in the past few years. All because You asked me to sit and be still. Thank You for asking me. Thank You for bringing me out of Egypt and for showing me You are my God. Thank You for being patient with me. For demonstrating Your love over and over to me. I know I have a lot more to learn about You. My thoughts, words, actions and appearance will be made new by You. I pray for my mind and heart to submit to You in this process. Amen.

Stand by Me

I could waste more time questioning why God asked me to write a book. I could waste more time doubting, worrying, wondering, whining and running away from the idea. Or I could enter in fully, 100%, and submit.

Every time I sit down to write now my belly gets really funny feeling. Anxious, nervous, sickish, and overwhelmed.

I know I must keep going, but to push past those feelings is more than I think I can do.

This morning I 'noticed' a new book that came out on Amazon and so I went to read what it was about. It sounded like a neat perspective on a controversial topic. I kept reading and then I noticed people had reviewed it. And this is where I made a 'not so good' choice and headed down a dark path. I read a '1 star' review of the book. Not smart.

My belly is all-sickish.

Writing is safe for me, because right now it's all 'protected' on my little laptop. But what if someday someone else reads it and they don't like it and then they put it in the '1 star' category too!

My belly is way nervous.

The end of James 1 says,

Keep oneself from being polluted by the world.

I am driving down the street this morning and my little guy is in the back in his car seat pretending to be Spider Man shooting webs. I am trying to not focus on what the world will say about what God has asked of me.

He so graciously reminds me that no matter where I am, He is there, standing beside me. Holding my hand. Lifting my chin. Breathing life into me. Filling me. Strengthening me. He is standing by me.

So do not fear, for I am with you; do not be dismayed, for I am
your God. I will strengthen you and help you; I will uphold
you with my righteous right hand. Isaiah 41:10

I will uphold you.
A power that enables me to stand.
Stand. Strength.

Just as long as you stand, stand by me.[1]

Now it is God who makes both us and you stand firm in Christ. He anointed
us, set His seal of ownership on us, and put His Spirit in our hearts as
a deposit, guaranteeing what is to come. 2 Corinthians 1:21-22

Yesterday a friend and I went for a run; it had been awhile since I had ran. It was great to be out there. The main thing I noticed was that I was very aware of my core. The core I have worked on finding in Pilates and Yoga.
A healthy core supports the body.
He breathes love into me. God is filling me with Himself. Love.
Love is the strong and healthy core that enables me to stand.
I stand in Jesus.

He entered heaven itself now to appear for us in God's presence. Hebrews 9:24

My Prayer: You are holy and righteous. Jesus, Your name is what redirects me and realigns me. You entered heaven for me. You went to God on my behalf. It is not me standing before God. Love represents me - to God. God sees a cleansed daughter through the filter of love! Truly knowing I am loved is based on God, the unchangeable, not on me and my emotions, thoughts or feelings. Knowing I am loved is accepting who God is, not who I think He is! Thank You for bringing Your will down to earth, from its Holy place of creation. You are mighty, powerful, and in total control. May my heart completely grasp and trust that. I love You Lord. Amen.

I Do

Nichole, please accept My words, 'I love you' and let them settle in your heart, let them change you." - God.

For years I wanted to know, truly know, that I was loved. Loved in spite of who I was, the mistakes I had made or would still make. The one thing I wanted to know was that I was loved. Truly, purely and unconditionally loved.

But to let you know the depth of my love for you. 2 Corinthians 2:4

Depth. Sinking in. Going to the deepest part. Continuing on. Enduring. Love.

For many years I 'knew' in my head that the Bible said Jesus loves me. I heard Sunday School teachers and preachers tell me. I went around in my 'head' knowing Jesus loves me.

I didn't do my hair yesterday. We were not dressed in our perfect matching Easter Sunday outfits. Nope, rather we all had jeans on. There was no Easter family photo of all of us dressed in our bright colored shirts. We walked in. Was it out of obligation? What do you do on Easter Sunday? Go to church.

I very felt uncomfortable, my heart and mind were not there.

My grandma was dying.

My daddy's heart was hurting.

As the rest of the church was singing about being alive and victory over death my heart was devastated… my grandma was dying.

For me death was stinging. Death was taking my grandma.

Selfish? Yes.

However I am human, and I was in pain. This hurt.

As I sat there on a pew and the tears came quickly the boys, all three of them, surrounded me and held on tight.

They were a tangible presence of my God.

For happy wasn't something I was feeling.

To hear the pastor say that people die and that it's all going to happen to us.

Yeah it's a fact. I know it's true, but there is a gap in our minds and hearts. I feel way more with my heart than I think with my head.

Is it a fault?

I don't know.

Despite the regrets, pain, sorrow, doubts, fears, worries, questions that I have; God is God.

God can take ALL things and make them into something good.

And we know that in all things God works for the good of those who know Him, who have been called according to His purpose. Romans 8:28

He can take death. And bring victory and life.

I'm just not seeing it or feeling it yet, and my Jesus, He is patient with me and He says it's okay.

He will wait.

He knew church would be hard yesterday.

He knew it wouldn't be the happiest Easter.

He knew and He is loving me through it!

I find myself in the Word in 1 John 4 and I read this:

And so we know and rely on the love God has for us. 1 John 4:16a

This verse is HUGE. How many times have I read this verse and say, "Yeah-yeah" and hope it brings warm fuzzy feelings? To know it is to experience it, to live it. Not try to justify it, understand it, explain it, earn it, and make it all add up. To rely on it means we can have nothing else in the way. A rock climber has to 'rely' on his ropes to secure him, hold him, save him, and keep him. This love has to be tested and lived in so we know to rely on it.

God met me on the pew in church on Easter Sunday while I was struggling, crying, grieving, questioning, worrying, and doubting. God was with me. He was holding on tight to me. There was purpose for this moment. He knew the exact time my heart needed to get to this point, to hear Him ask;

"Nichole, do you know I love you?"

He knew the exact time my heart would 'feel love'.

Mascara was running down my face and I couldn't sing the songs about being alive. My grandma was dying. But it was in these moments that I felt and knew God loved me. For real! For the first time!

Was it because I hadn't created a barrier in my attempt to 'try' and be in control?

God loves me. Unconditionally. Not because of who I am, but because of who He is. He has opened my heart wide and dumped His GREAT love on me.

On this Easter Sunday I knew in my heart for the first time that God loved me unconditionally. While I was struggling with losing my Grandma, God was filling the void with Himself.

"Nichole, do you know I love you?"

There it is, the question God was asking, "Do you know I love you?"

Maybe He's not asking a rhetorical question. Maybe I am to answer it.

"Nichole, do you know I love you?"

It's amazing how things come to you. I woke up with a chapter title rolling around in my head. *I Do.* I jumped in the shower thinking about those two words. What do they mean? After all these months of God stressing for me to just be, what in the world did *I Do* mean? *I Do* what? In the middle of the shower I got it. It was my answer to the question He has been asking. It was the answer to the question in bold letters on the front cover of this book. It was the answer He has brought me to.

"I Do".

I do know He loves me. Right? Don't I? Isn't that what this journey has been all about? How do I know? Time spent in relationship. Questions asked. Life lived. Stuff taken away. Control loosened. Stillness and comfort ushered in. Joy and contentment. This I know, He loves me. I do. I stand strong face to face with my Creator, legs feel the connection to the earth, shoulders are relaxed and down, core engaged, chin parallel to the floor, neck soft, eyes gazing forward. I am here in His presence; I am loved. Not because of who I am, but because of who He is. He brought me to this point. He is patient. He is good. He is faithful. He is Love.

Only God can take a horrible, no good very bad day on Easter Sunday in church and bring something so beautiful out of it. Only God could take the very hard moments of my grandma dying to get me to **know** He loves me. I can't help but smile and wonder if God orchestrated my grandma's very life so I would know, truly know His love for me.

You satisfy me with Your love.[1]

I sang those words yesterday in church. It wasn't the first time I had seen those words and it wasn't the first time I sang those words.

However, something was different yesterday. When I sang them yesterday I meant them. I meant them because I have lived them. I have had to. I have had to come to a place of complete knowing that nothing, nothing else will satisfy me.

You satisfy me with Your love.

Satisfaction comes from knowing and experiencing the true thing; LOVE, in comparison to all the false idols that I tried to shove/cram into the void.

I have tried. I have worked hard.

I have eaten to try to satisfy.

I have gotten married to satisfy others and myself.

I have performed on a stage to satisfy.

I have dressed to satisfy.

I have gone shopping over and over and over to satisfy.

I have kept friends and unhealthy relationships going to try to satisfy my needs.

The list could go on and on.

Just reading the above makes me feel tired and to think I had lived like that for years! Living a life in which I was trying to control, trying so hard to satisfy. Trying to satisfy myself.

I will refresh the weary and **satisfy** *the faint.*
Jeremiah 31:25 (emphasis added)

Weary and faint don't even seem like 'big' enough words to describe my exhaustion.

So what clicked for me? How did I finally get it? How did that feeling of complete peace and contentment come yesterday while singing those words?

I allowed Him to love me.

You open your hand and **satisfy** *the desires of every*
living thing. Psalm 145:16 (emphasis added)

Because I know that You love me²

It felt so good to write yesterday. I think what I enjoyed the most was just being reminded of God's faithful presence in my life. I also can see His love for me. I am reading *Heaven Is for Real*[3] and the author is talking about how hearing something and knowing it are two totally different things. I had heard Jesus loves me. I heard it sung at church, I had sung the song myself, I had sung the song to the boys, I heard it from sermons, from speakers, from music on the radio. I had heard it many times. Now I know God loves me. He loves me.

Learning that God loves me, that's what this whole season has been about. There is importance in stating that I didn't fully know He loved me when I gave my life to Him at the age of 13. I didn't fully know it until I was in my 30's. I didn't know God loved me just by going to church, or Sunday School, or by singing songs, or memorizing Scripture. Learning that God loves me was not a onetime event. It was a process, a journey, better yet it was a relationship. A relationship lived daily.

"Yes Lord, I know You love me! You love me unconditionally all the time! You love me in spite of me, because of who You are. Your love is right, fulfilling, peaceful and perfect. Your love is just what I was created for. Amen"

Learning I am loved by God was more than learning church doctrine. More than walking through the door. For some will come to learn they are loved by their Creator in a building called a church. Some won't.

Have you ever lost something? Or has something been taken away and then you realized just how great it was?

Do you have regrets of things you should have said? Or should have done? Do you wish you could have used your time more wisely?

Losing my grandma has been hard.

She was a great woman.

A woman who had a whole lotta strength, courage, patience, grace and love.

She listened more than she spoke.

I wish I had known her more. I wish I could have been there more.

However, the reality is that I can't turn back the clock.

Oh speaking of clocks, Grandma had one of those chiming hour clocks that every hour and every half hour it would chime… through the night! It is now hanging on the wall at my parents' house. (Oh and Mom and Dad I am okay if I *don't* inherit that next!)

What I would give to spend one more hour standing at her kitchen sink getting the dishes washed with her.

I would tell her I love her.

I would tell her thank you for my daddy.

I would love to be sitting at the kitchen table and sitting in the chair that was by the green phone that hung on the wall.

I have some forever great memories of Grandma. I have her Chex Mix recipe and her silverware.

Yesterday I got more from Grandma then I ever thought I would.

God revealed to me her purpose here on earth… or at least a glimpse of it.

For Grandma's purpose was to show this earth what it means to give grace. To the very end.

To love when it's hard. To be completely unselfish.

"Grandma I am listening. I hear your precious last words. I will never forget you, but most importantly, I will live this life on purpose and take to heart your message so softly but boldly spoken."

Grandma I love you!

My Prayer: Love. Finding the true source. How humbling it is to know that You would be so patient and understanding with me. That the Lover of my soul allowed each moment to unfold. To build trust, to smother me with grace, to strengthen our relationship. So I could learn Your voice, so I would hold tight to Your hand. So I would know my place in You. So I could answer Your question, "Do you know I love you?" I do. I can shout it victoriously. I do. I do know You love me. I know because You pursued me. I know because You stayed. I know because You listened, You answered, You held on tight when I wanted to let go. I know because You spoke boldly to me. You corrected me, disciplined me, and picked me up. You accepted me each and every moment. You smiled upon me; You laughed with me and at me. You loved me continually. You reached out, You caught my tears, You filled me with strength, energy, courage, patience, peace, joy, contentment. You shined light into darkness, You highlighted the truth. You repeated often Your love for me. You let me question, but quickly reassured with answers. Thank You, Amen.

Focus/Balance/Transition

On Tuesday afternoon I was helping to coach soccer practice. I was leading the dribble drill around the field when I rolled my ankle. There was a loud popping sound in my ankle followed by some 'owie' pain and swelling. I popped in some ibuprofen and sat out the rest of the practice with an ice bag on my ankle. Knowing I would be back coaching very soon. I would be fine.

I walked around on it for a week.

Okay I limped around on it, but I was getting around! I was not able to go on my runs, which was causing me a whole lot of frustration and internal disappointment. I was thinking it was fine and it would heal. In reality I was doing more damage by walking around on it. Am I seeing a correlation to not allowing our body to rest and heal fully; not acknowledging our need to sit out and heal?

The next Tuesday at soccer practice my doctor friend, who noticed I hadn't been at the morning runs with the Runner Girls, showed up and put my ankle in an Aircast and sent me for x-rays. The pictures of my ankle revealed a very bad sprain and torn ligaments. It needed to be restricted and held together to heal and I needed to rest it as much as possible.

Rest, which meant I was still not able to run.

I don't like to be restricted or told to slow down. It's like being told to sit down and be still all over again. How did I get back here?

I find myself back on the bench. My ankle needed to heal.

One would think that I had this 'sitting it out' thing down to a fine art by now.

One would think that I knew I needed to take the time to heal properly.

One would think that this paralleled the story I was writing in a book!

But I was fighting the healing process. Again?

I was fighting not being in control. Again?

I was fighting the fact that I had to give up running.

I was supposed to be resting, but instead I was pouting, whining, and fighting God.

I was bummed about giving up running, to the point that I even said these words:

"I can't have the **one thing** that helps me with life."

My human heart revealed in that moment that running was the one thing that helped me do life.

I definitely had some things a little out of order.

Some perspective came in the form of the sermon yesterday at church, when Pastor preached the words, "Joy doesn't come from physical health."

I resisted the urge to stand up and shout back, "You wanna bet?"

My God 'should be' the one the thing that gets me through life, but my girlie human heart sometimes gets things out of order. And my stubborn self needs a BIG wake up call.

I want to be running.

I don't want to take the time to rest and heal.

I don't want to sit any longer.

And I most definitely don't want to write a book that I can't write.

I feel like He is asking too much.

Knowing that God knew this would happen. His love will stop at nothing to get our attention!

I press on toward the goal. Philippians 3:14

I can think of many examples right now of 'pressing on.' Pressing on through PT to heal my ankle so I can go back out and run; pressing on when I am tired and worn out and want a break; pressing on in the busy schedule of everyday life as a wife and momma; pressing on to keep writing the book.

Still running! Not physically as my ankle is a little messed up right now. But emotionally and mentally, I am still running. I have allowed myself to become distracted and thus not obey. I wish I could say that I am the good obedient girl who has 'finished' writing this book. But nope! I am still begging God to take it away. I have considered what if I just don't do it. What if I ignore the whole thing? I spoke that out loud to The Engineer yesterday right here in our bedroom, and with his arms wrapped around me and his eyes intently looking at me he said, "Nichole please don't do that to our family or yourself."

But what about all the people who are ignoring their purpose or calling?

My head truly hurts right now. If I could opt out I would. I would let it go and walk away. But there is something deep inside me right now that knows beyond a doubt, that there is someone who needs to know Jesus loves them.

The process of writing this book is such a parallel to my life story - running and not being still. Not wanting to feel the pain the 'owies'. Not trusting God to love me.

I want to know what to do. I want to know how to write. I want it to be right.

Will I ever get this? Will I ever quit fighting?

Don't writers whip out there books much faster than this? Don't writers enjoy writing? Isn't it something they want to do?

Today I came across someone's blog and she stated, "Writing is therapy" I smile and laugh out loud. Really? It feels more like torture to me. To be writing I have to be sitting, quiet and away from people.

All things that I don't like! And here in this past month I am learning God will get His way. He's in control. I am learning what 100% submission looks like. I am sorry to say it wasn't voluntary. Nope. Rather forced. I am thankful He got my attention. And I am thankful for the healing that is taking place.

Healing in writing?

Could it be Lord that this was part of Your plan and process all along? The thought just came to me, really? Now that's some crazy love!

Writing is utter solitude, the descent into the cold abyss of oneself.[1]

I think one of the reasons I am 'fighting' the writing process is because I don't like being alone. I don't like the feeling of loneliness. And yet even as I type these words I hear…

"You are not alone Nichole. I am with you. And that was part of the process. To get you to know Me. My presence, My love, that I am everything you need."

I doubt and question - why me? Help me not to waste God's time. I am so afraid. I am SO unsure of what I am doing! It's not a writer's block… I would have to be a writer… HA! I don't have a stinkin' clue how this book is going to physically look. What will the cover be? How many chapters? What titles? What words? Length?

My Creator whispers,

"What do I look like Nichole? Focus on Me. Fix your eyes on Me."

To stay focused is difficult for me. Especially during yoga! The focus during yoga should be on the breath. My mind is busy entertaining anything but my breath. I am becoming aware of the chaos and stress that comes with a full chaotic mind full of bouncing thoughts. This chaos and stress is the opposite of peace and contentment. Life feels out of sorts and completely out of balance.

It's easy to stay balanced while sitting, but to balance while standing you need some help. One of the things they teach in yoga when attempting poses that require more balance (like tree pose, or standing eagle pose), is to have a focal point. The yogis call it a 'drishti'. This focal point can be a fixed point out in front of you to focus your eyes on. This grounds you. It allows you to find more balance.

For God is not a God of disorder but of peace. 1 Corinthians 14:33

I suffer from 'chaotic thinking' allowing too many things to buzz around in my head. I need help to focus, breathe and live in this moment.

I know I need balance in my life. The benefits of this balance are peace and contentment.

I need a fixed focal point.

I am guilty of fixing my focus on myself.

I am also seemed to be focused on someone else's journey at many times.

For balance cannot be truly held and maintained when our eyes are distracted by something or someone else. Like holding a yoga pose. I am way more balanced when my focus, my breath, my intent are on my pose and not that of the person practicing next me.

Other times I have no idea what I am focused on because I haven't paused long enough to figure it out, because I was too busy running.

Where is my focus?

*Therefore, since we are surrounded by such a great cloud of witnesses, let us throw off everything that hinders and the sin that so easily entangles. And let us run with perseverance the race marked out for us, **fixing our eyes on Jesus**, the pioneer and perfecter of faith. For the joy set before him he endured the cross, scorning its shame, and sat down at the right hand of the throne of God. Consider him who endured such opposition from sinners, so that you will not grow weary and lose heart. Hebrews 12:1-3 (emphasis mine)*

When I get in the way things start to blur, get messy and don't feel balanced.

I need His strength to adjust. My little stubborn eyes can stay focused on the wrong thing and sometimes I just need my Jesus to grab my little chin and tilt my gaze!

I need to fix my eyes on Jesus.

He needs to be the focal point.

When I am focused on Him I will find balance.

Keep my eyes fixed on Him. And the things of this world will grow strangely dim.

Finding balance in God will bring peace and contentment.

This morning as I was brushing my teeth, I looked into my closest and saw the shoe box up on the top shelf... *new balance...* my shoes are speaking to me! God will use anything to get our attention. And blessed be its shoes!

I will make peace your governor and righteousness your ruler.
Isaiah 60:17b

I can sense this as the scale of balance. For when I am getting stressed, upset, easily angered, annoyed, jealous, lonely or any of my old human characteristics, I am out of balance. Fixing my gaze on Him. Each inhale and exhale. Balance.

I need His balance. I need Him. I need His love. I need to live in that balance.

Balance in my thoughts. Be aware of what I am thinking about, and to fill my thoughts with life giving positive ones.

Balance in my words. A time to be silent and a time to speak. Listen MORE. Speak LESS.

Balance in my actions. What am I spending my time doing? Who is it benefiting?

God is within her, she will not fall; God will help her at break of day.
Psalm 46:5

I have not arrived. I remember the days when it was so easy for me to cry out, "Are we there yet Lord?" I felt like I had been through enough. For my focus was on the pain, hurt and misery of the restoration and healing. My focus was on the 'yuck' coming off of me.

"I love you Nichole. You are My daughter and I see you and care for you. I am all you need. I am to be your center. Your point of grounding. Hear Me. Listen to My voice. Trust Me. Know that I am peace, joy, love, grace, mercy. I am what you need. Nothing more."

As I snuggled into bed last night I felt God loving on me. Speaking right to my heart. Whispers of encouragement, confirmation, assurance. Reminding me to stand strong and hold on tight to His hand. There is peace filling my mind and heart. A peace that confirms God knows and it's all right. Everything is all right. This season of life is all right. To be focused and fixed on Him. With my eyes, mind and heart. That my life will come into balance when God is the focal point. My mind and heart are full. I remember falling asleep last night knowing, truly knowing for the first time in my life, what His peace feels like. A peace that answers questions, a peace that calms me. A peace that says it's okay for me to have unknowns. A peace that assures me that God is with me.

My lover spoke and said to me, "Arise, my darling, my
beautiful one, and come with me Song of Songs 2:13b

May I trust fully in the future steps You are asking me to take.

Standing, standing,
Standing on the promises of God my Savior;
Standing, standing,
I'm standing on the promises of God.[2]

I am able now to look back and see that God didn't want to punish me. He asked me to be still for a period of time so that He could help me focus on Him. So that I could learn that He is the most important and must be my focal point.

Calming the mind, bringing ourselves to a place where we can see what is right before us. I am here. Typing at this keyboard with my Jesus. He who believes I can do all things, because He is in me. I hear the sound of the dishwasher scrubbing the dishes from the breakfast I shared with my boys. I see my brown-eyed girl dog enjoying a dream as she lays on the carpet to the side of me. The smell of daddy's cologne in our home because two boys wanted to smell good like daddy does before they headed off to school. My fingers on the keyboard, revealing the message of my heart. Being aware isn't about striving or trying, I am realizing it's about being. Being aware. There is calmness and peace here. There is balance here.

And I know there can be
No greater love
Than this.[3]

My Prayer: I am not broken or ruined beyond Your repair. Thank You for loving me so much and not allowing me to settle. I am holding tightly to Your hand. I desire to keep my eyes fixed on You. Knowing that the work You started in me You will complete. Help me to learn Your rhythm and balance for my life. Fix my eyes on You, my ears to Your voice, my hand tightly to Yours. Commit to walk forward. Amen.

PART 3

Walk

Walk This Way

Walk. Each step we take is a choice. Steady. Set pace. Rhythm. This is active. Moving forward. Faith, trust, and obedience are needed to make healthy choices; these will lead to the right steps taken.

Ellie and I just returned from our walk around 'the block'. The sun was shining and it was warm outside. The lilacs are blooming and when the breeze blows you can take in the amazing smell. Usually she pulls for the first 10 minutes or so, as if she was taking me on a walk. I keep pulling back on the leash and repeating the words, "walk with me." Ellie hardly pulled her leash today on the walk. Maybe she's getting the hang of 'the walk'. Then at about 10 minutes into the walk I notice she is walking in step with me and no longer pulling. To which I praise her saying, "Good girl; good walk."

Will I get the hang of this walk with Him?

"Walk with Me."

My evidence of need for Him is strong. My weakness needs His strength.

> *His pleasure is not in the strength of the horse, nor his delight in the legs of a man; the LORD delights in those who fear him, who put their hope in his unfailing love. Psalm 147:10-11*

There is a wonderful simplicity, boldness and straightforwardness in this verse. Again the reminder comes. This is not about me. Not something I can figure out. Not in what I can think, say or do. I am to put my hope in Him - His unfailing love. My hope needs to be in love. His perfect, unfailing, consistent, enduring, pure, righteous, holy, grace filled, LOVE!

But the man who looks intently into the perfect law that gives freedom, and continues to do this, not forgetting what he had heard, but doing it - he will be blessed in what he does. James 1:25

What I am hearing when I read the above verse;

"Nichole look intently to Me, hear My voice, continue to seek Me, continue to know Me. Don't forget about what I have said to you, what I have taught you, do what I have asked. Rely on Me for all you need, including self-control. Honor Me Nichole in all you say and do, and you will be blessed."

May I be aware! Aware of how blessed I am to see, hear, feel and do. How blessed I am to be known by God, to be loved by Him, to be in relationship with Him. How blessed to be able to write. Wow. What did I just type? I think it's about getting past what I can and cannot do, and trusting what God can do. Allowing myself to be humbled. To submit. Because what comes out of us is the testimony of what resides in us. For He has been working to clean, purify, heal and restore that which was so broken. I have always wanted to represent Him well, but its way more authentic when God represents Himself. When I get out of the way. Sit down. Be still and allow God to do what He has wanted to do for years. Love me. Love me down to the depths. The places I didn't think He would want to go. *Father, forgive me.* His willingness to go, to stay, to continue on. Relationship. I am learning so much and it feels like more than I will be able to retain. So I choose to trust. That it won't be lost, but invested. Soaked into the places that need it. Learning I am not to manipulate the process to fulfill my comfort levels, but to allow the process to mess with them. To not waste time questioning that which I don't understand, but to trust that God will inform if and when need be. For the problem doesn't reside in the question, but the allowance of the distraction. To move forward in relationship regardless of my readiness, for that is testimony of faith and trust in God. Not allowing my emotions to dictate our relationship. Huge! I am not in control. I can't and won't ever change Him. He loves me.

Before I knew your name
You knew my every breath
Before I found my way
You knew my every step
Before I knew everything that I need
You gave it all to me.[1]

As I am waking up for the day I head out to the back porch to let my Ellie girl outside. I step onto the back porch - it smelled different. Different good.

I had walked into something different. I had taken steps and there was something inside me that felt so good about it. Felt right.

You see I truly believe that I had to leave Egypt.

Do not conform any longer to the pattern of this world. Romans 12:2a

These powerful words hold such instruction, challenge, hope and purpose. The Word, it loves on me, pours grace on me, teaches me, corrects me, convicts me, leads and guides me, and encourages me to keep walking in step with Him. I pray I will remember that nothing this world has to offer will fill a void, desire, or need in me. I also am not to behave or act like the 'pattern' of this world. I am not able to do this in my own strength or will, but in Him all things are possible. I want to stay in step with Him.

To keep my eyes focused on Him and Him alone. I know the struggle with people pleasing and I know for years it held me captive in Egypt. I am learning I wasn't created to live in captivity. Rather I was made to live in a Promised Land filled full of abundant life, and that's where I want my feet going. So I take one step at a time and I hold on tight to His hand.

The Bible is filled with real people who lived in relationship with God.

Their relationship with Him allowed Him to work in them and through them.

But Noah found favor in the eyes of the LORD. Noah was a righteous man, blameless among the people of his time, and he walked with God. Genesis 6:8-9

Noah started in relationship with God. In that relationship Noah learned who God was. He learned how to listen, how to trust, and how to obey. So that when God asked him to build a boat Noah was able to obey because of his great love and respect for God.

In Exodus 3 and 4 we see God choose Moses to be the leader of His people. Moses didn't prepare for years on how to be a leader. I believe Moses in all his humanness said yes to God and then allowed God to work through him.

Then there is David, not even his own family thought him worthy of being a king. (1 Samuel 16) But God knew David was a man after His heart. (Acts 13:22)

The book of Esther shares a beautiful story of a woman who was obedient and allowed her God to use her, and that is just what He did, in His perfect timing and way. I don't think Esther knew all that her title, as queen of Persia, would entail. But she trusted and loved her God.

Oh and if we dare think that we have to get this whole relationship with Him mastered before He chooses us or uses us? Think again!

As Jesus went on from there, he saw a man named Matthew sitting at the tax collector's booth.

"Follow me," he told him, and Matthew got up and followed him. Matthew 9:9

I don't think Matthew was sitting there preparing for Jesus to walk by. But I do believe that Matthew's getting up and saying yes was the best decision he ever made.

Also Mary, another one of God's girls.

*But the angel said to her, "Do not be afraid, Mary, you
have found favor with God." Luke 1:30*

How did she find favor with God? Just being, being in relationship with Him.

So, because of that relationship He was able to find her willing to be used by Him.

*"I am the Lord's servant," Mary answered. "May it
be to me as you have said." Luke 1:38.*

I am grateful for those who have walked this journey before me. Their footsteps show they stayed close to Him. They knew Him. They communicated with Him. They depended on Him.

I desire to intentionally walk forward in Him.

*If they had been thinking of the country they had left, they
would have had opportunity to return. Hebrews 11:15*

I remember thinking last night as I fell asleep, how far out of Egypt I have truly come. How I am 'better' (celebrate progress) at coming and seeking Him. Less void filling more Jesus seeking. How the 'feelings' of wanting to run seem less frequent. The need to go out and buy and shop not on my mind as much. I still feel weak in areas of food and eating. There will always be an aspect of weakness as to not forget the 'feeling' of 'need', so I remember to seek Him.

May the Lord direct your hearts into God's love and Christ's perseverance. 2 Thessalonians 3:5

And the idols will totally disappear. Isaiah 2:18

These words are hitting me hard this morning for I am really good at creating idols. Anything that takes the place of God! Filling the void with something other than Him.

No longer will they follow the stubbornness of their own hearts Jeremiah 3:17b

I am not my feelings and emotions. I desperately want to be in control and 'fix' me. However I can't. God is working, cleaning up, peeling off, repairing, and renewing me in every area. Though the journey is tough, overwhelming, not completely understood, I know He is in control and so I will keep walking this way. To be perfectly honest I can't take the steps, I am pushed and prodded by Him. So many times I have chosen to walk my own way.

When God called me to come and sit with Him I wasn't completely sure about faith or trusting Him. I was still focused on myself. I am learning to put my faith in Him. To trust that He knows the best for me. With God's amazing patience and love I am learning that I was made to be loved. Loved by Him.

But if from there you seek the Lord your God, you will find him if you seek him with all your heart and with all your soul. Deuteronomy 4:29

Direction and guidance come from God. Without God I stumble.

I will instruct you and teach you in the way you should go;
I will counsel you with my loving eye on you. Psalm 32:8

I am sitting here at my laptop. I have two hours on the timer. I have scheduled this time to write. Scary huh? I feel so overwhelmed and out of my league! I need to write. I am scheduled to write. Trying to justify this time to myself let alone anyone else, seems so hard. I sit in a house right now that has many things that need to be done. The dishes are stacked, the dishwasher needs emptying, the laundry needs washed, beds need to be made, and the back porch needs sweeping. All these things are competing for my attention and time. I allow them to because I don't 'feel' worthy or capable of writing this book. Why do I fight it? Why do I think it's not possible? Seriously, who wants to read a book about a girl who struggled being obedient, who struggled with the idea that she was loved by God?

Am I the only one who has struggled with the knowing that God loves me?

Deep in my soul there is a voice that whispers, "No daughter there are more, many more people who are dying, dying to know they are loved. Dying to know they are precious, adored, and worth it. There are more people dying to know that I think the world of them. Dying to live free in the grace, and love I have for them."

It's that voice that urges me on to do what He has asked me to do. The voice that pushes me through the fear of the unknowns. The fear of an editor critiquing and red marking up the whole thing. I go forward for the one who will someday be holding this book and hears for the first time in their heart, truly hears, that God loves them.

My Prayer: Thank You for this season of learning to walk with You. I want to know Your Word more, I want to build faith, to strengthen my perseverance, trust You more, to learn to pray without ceasing, I want pure thoughts, and I want self- control.

But Lord MORE than anything, I want You. I want to know Your characteristics as my God because I experience them. Lord as I type this I know with this wanting comes 'a need to live it out'. Help me know this is NOT about earning, striving or doing it myself. Please forgive me for allowing distractions to take my eyes off You. To keep relinquishing control to You Lord. To trust and know You are God. You are good and everything You do is good. You and You alone are the definition of me. May I submit even more in this Lord. May the peace and calmness I feel and know now as I sit here and type be the constant thing, may it be my balance point. So that when I get myself too far off, I know to search for this. To search for You, my place. May the very things I want be what You created for me. May the desires of my heart be Your perfect will. Each day to see and know You more. Thank You Lord for Your love that has captured my mind, heart and soul. May I know it, truly know it. Amen.

More Than Words

Actions speak louder than words. Today as I am writing, I'm thinking about how to 'prove' His love for me, for us, for the world. How do I write and prove it to people? As I type this sentence I realize it's not my job. He hasn't asked me to prove anything. Rather I think love reveals itself. The process of revealing is way more genuine and graceful. Revealing takes time. It takes awareness.

What is there to be aware of? What has God done to show His love for us?

God Created - the world and all the beauty around us. Mountains that reach up to the sky, snow that falls softly, trees whose leaves blow in the wind, rivers that go and go and go, birds that soar, children who giggle and laugh. We see sunrises that come at just the right time and sunsets that color the sky perfectly, the coast that competes with no other as far as sound, sight and smell. People created in His image. People revealing joy, love, compassion.

God Came - to earth, to live with His people, knowing full well who we were and how we behaved. He came to experience and have emotions in the form of a human, He spent time, sharing, giving and serving. He came to make relationships with us possible.

God Carried a Cross - to bridge a gap between us here on earth, and God in heaven. He knew the cost and He chose compassion. His selfless act restored the ultimate mess we made so we could return to our original intent and design, to be in a grace and love filled relationship with our Creator.

God Continues - to love, give grace, restore, redeem, heal, create, and remind us that we need Him, to have patience, and to teach us. He continues to pursue us.

Jesus was 30 years old before He started His ministry, a ministry that would last three years. He did a whole lotta work in these three years. He packed in a whole lot of teaching, healing and loving on people.

Jesus' purpose was to bring God to the people. He came to restore a relationship that just couldn't be fixed by the law of the Old Testament. He came to be the void filler.

During the three years of His ministry Jesus met people right where they were.

The disciples on the shores with their fishing boats.

A tax collector at work with his tax paperwork.

A woman whose past was the talk of the town.

Jesus came to where they were. Jesus came to bring them a grace and loved filled relationship. He came to meet them where they were to bring them closer to the Father.

He came to meet with me. To remind me of His love for me.

God told **me:**

"I've never quit loving you and never will.
Expect love, love, and more love!" Jeremiah 31:3 (The Message)

As God and I have talked over the past few days He has showed me that my healing was something He would do, but that I can't limit His ways or His timetable.

He says:

"Have faith in God," Jesus answered. "I tell you the truth, if anyone says to this mountain, 'Go, throw yourself into the sea,' and does not doubt in his heart but believes that what he says will happen, it will be done for him." Mark 11:22-23

I say:

"My faith is in You God. I know You are mighty and capable of anything. I want to be used so that you receive all the glory and honor. I am willing to submit my life."

"What is more pleasing to the Lord:
your burnt offerings and sacrifices
or your obedience to his voice?
Listen! Obedience is better than sacrifice,
and submission is better than offering the fat of rams."
1 Samuel 15:22 (New Living Translation)

So I have no livestock. Which God is fully aware of. But I am sure He has something in there for me.

I hear God telling me, "Nichole I don't want a ritual sacrifice from you. I want a love relationship with you. One where I bring you closer to my heart and out of love for me, you will obey. Bringing you closer to my heart Nichole means things have to go that are blocking our relationship."

So what am I to do now? Are there steps? Rules? Is there a way to make this all work out? I find myself in the pattern of wanting to get this whole thing figured out.

How foolish can you be? After starting your Christian lives in the Spirit, why are you now trying to become perfect by your own human effort? Have you experienced so much for nothing? Surely it was not in vain, was it? I ask you again, does God give you the Holy Spirit and work miracles among you because you obey the law? Of course not! It is because you believe the message you heard about Christ. Galatians 3:3-5 (New Living Translation)

Is it about following rules?

Team Hamblin tries to focus on relationships over rules. We try to see the person first. I don't want to be more focused on rules with my boys. I want to build a relationship with them, so that out of love, obedience will come.

Relationship. Love. Obedience.

I want to be in a relationship with my God. I want Him in every detail of my life, so that I know Him intimately. A relationship is more than being saved. A relationship with Jesus means you not only have asked Jesus to be your Savior you have also invited Him to be your Lord.

It's more than being saved.

There is embarrassment in being a Christian (one who follows Jesus Christ) for years without truly knowing Jesus loved me. Yes I sang the song, but I didn't believe the words. *'Jesus loves me.'*

It's more than words.

'For it is not mere words that nourish the soul, but God Himself, and unless and until the hearers find God in personal experience they are not the better for having heard the truth. The Bible is not an end in itself, but a means to bring men to an intimate and satisfying knowledge of God, that they many enter into Him, that they may delight in His Presence, may taste and know the inner sweetness of the very God Himself in the core and center of their hearts.'[1]

There was a time when it was easier for me to tell you that Jesus loved you. I believed every bit of it. He loved you. He adored you. He treasured you. You were His. I believed it. I enjoyed blogging about it, I enjoyed speaking about it, and I really enjoyed telling you face to face. I still believe He loves you. He adores and treasures you, because you are His! Created on purpose for Him to love and treasure and adore. The new part I have learned that this is all true for me too. I know you might be thinking and wondering how in the world a girl could say all this when she never really knew it for herself. I know crazy huh? Talk about a hypocrite. I know! It was easier for me that way. I kept God at a distance from myself, so as to be in control and so He wouldn't waste His time on me. It felt much easier to encourage others with the love of Jesus, but oh so stinkin' difficult and overwhelming to allow it for myself. Weird? I know it's truly difficult for me to wrap my head and heart around all this.

It's taken a few years on this close and personal relationship with my Jesus to start to figure this all out. And really 'figure out' are not the right words. I am lacking the right words right now. Something started to change when I started sitting still and hearing Him. I got to a point where I had nothing to do but listen. Funny how He always trumps the stubborn strong headed girlie in me. Jesus loves me. It was more than words of a Sunday school song; it was more than words. Do you remember that 8th grade song, okay it was 8th grade for me, 'More Than Words'[2] by Extreme? That song was played at every dance and all of us girls were desperately hoping to be chosen to dance to this song.

However I digress, easily! Over the past few years I realized in the big and little things His love was not just a phrase to throw out. His love is not dependent on who I am, what I have done or will do. He has shown His love in many big ways, small ways, and silly fun ways. I am sure there were moments He was definitely loving me and showing me just how much, and being human unfortunately I missed it. I can say that I am more intent today on finding Him and His love in each and every day.

More than words.
More than Bible reading - more than attending church.
Being in church as a little girl, giving my heart to Jesus at 13, and

going to church almost every Sunday since then, I know church rules, I know doctrines, and I know hymns, and none of that 'changed' me. I don't want to be **doing church**. I don't want to be numb and fill a spot on a pew. I don't want to limit myself to a building, a doctrine, or a style of worship.

It's a rainy Wednesday and God meets me while I am sitting at my dining room table amongst the ordinary to very clearly tell me…

"I love you Nichole."

I am aware of this love. It's always been here. It was an awareness in my head. But my running, fleeing, escaping and fear have kept me from fully knowing it. Knowing it in my heart. God has truly endured me on this amazing journey. A journey to find out who God is and to get to know Him. That's what relationships are, right? A process of learning about each other, but ultimately coming to know, really know I am loved. That's the whole game changer. Knowing that I am loved changes my heartbeat, my view, my way of doing life.

I want to be obedient to God. I want to be real with my Creator and give directly back to Him from my heart. I want to be passionate about who He is and who I am and live in that every minute. I want to be praising, and worshipping a God who is so amazing. I want to fall more in love with Him.

'Give me words, I'll misuse them

Obligations, I'll misplace them

Cuz all religion ever made of me

Was just a sinner with a stone tied to my feet

Its gotta be

More like falling in love

Than something to believe in." [8]

God is not asking me to get bogged down with getting it all right and knowing all the details, saying all the right things, attending the 'right' church, reading the right translation of the Bible.

He is asking me to live life with Him.

Be in relationship with Him.

Relationships take time. It is commitment to show up - to be there - to spend time with one another. When The Engineer and I started our relationship we spent time studying, going for car rides, eating the Walmart hot dog deal, watching '*ER*' on Thursday nights. We were in college when we met; we did what we could afford to do. Which budget wise meant we just spent time together. We talked and got to know each other.

Can you truly fall more in love with someone? Is falling in love a one-time thing? I don't think so. I know I am more in love with The Engineer than when I first married him. Our relationship has changed, we know each other more now, and we have weathered life together. We have strengthened our relationship, and through this I love him more. I am seeing my love for my boys grow too. The more I get to know their personalities the more I am falling in love with them.

Walking with Jesus. Each step is a choice. A steady pace and rhythm set by Him. This is active. Moving forward. I find myself being continually humbled. I praise God for that change and progress because it's a sign that God is working in me!

> '*God isn't keeping a record of each time we fall, but He is excited about our progress, and we should be excited, too!*'[4]

Religion versus Relationship.

> *The former regulation is set aside because it was weak and useless (for the law made nothing perfect), and a better hope is introduced, by which we draw near to God. Hebrews 7:18-19*

If that verse does not depict my life and me! Trying, striving, earning, and achieving. I am weak and my way is useless. Fancy me asking for God to save me, to become my Savior and then trying to earn it? I am learning His way is better.

Jesus was introduced. He is our better hope. He is how we draw near to God.

My Prayer: Thank You Lord for loving me in this very moment. Lord I pray that this will go into my heart by the power and working of the Holy Spirit. That my mind, thoughts, words, actions, and living will be honoring to You, and when it's not that I will be made aware and correct it. This is only possible because of Your love and grace for me. I pray that even though I know with my head that I am a work in progress and not complete, my heart feels the pain and struggle of the continual shifting and changing. It is unsettling and uncomfortable and purposeful and very right all at the same time. I praise You Lord for Your presence in my life. May I continue to become less and You More. May I continue in relationship with You. Amen.

Love's Been Following You

I can look back and see that love has followed me. There were many times that I was being pursued by love. Many times love came through family members and friends.

> *'I know sometimes it's hard to believe it*
> *But Love's been following you*
> *From where I stand I'm able to see it*
> *And Love's been following you.'*[1]

The Engineer's motto, *'leave things better than you find them'*, was passed onto him by his dad, and this is something he lives out. I am truly spoiled by him. Doors don't squeak, outlets are always nice and tight, pictures are hung properly on the wall, no leaky water faucets, drains drain, cars are maintained and clean, light bulbs are replaced the second they burn out, and vents are clean, air filters changed every three months. He tends to take care of things. It must just be that fabulous engineering DNA in him! Sometimes he fixes things and I don't realize they needed fixing until he's done with them, like my old laptop.

My laptop and I had worked out quite the routine. I would turn her on about 15 minutes before I needed to use her, knowing she needed the time to boot up and really be ready. I had learned she just needed to be in charge. She would decide which days she would open certain programs or not. Certain days the mouse would work. Other days the battery would not last longer than 20 minutes. She was in charge, and I just let her be. In walked The Engineer who is WAY MORE efficient with his time, I think he calls it lean management or something and, decided to love on me. He jumped on a website that you can order computer devices from and had one shipped right to our porch. Here I am typing on this new fast flash laptop. I do admit it is way less temperamental. Thank you Engineer for following me around and loving on me.

Long ago, even before he made the world, God chose us to be his very own through what Christ would do for us; he decided then to make us holy in his eyes, without a single fault—we who stand before him covered with his love. His unchanging plan has always been to adopt us into his own family by sending Jesus Christ to die for us. And he did this because he wanted to! Ephesians 1:4-5 (Living Bible)

Jesus has covered me with His love. That has got to be the best part of those verses! ***Covered with His love.*** Allowing this love, the perfect love to cover me and take over my life is living in the original plan of the Creator. Love does so many things if we allow it to.

The Lord came to us from far away, saying, "I have loved you with a love that lasts forever. So I have helped you come to Me with loving-kindness." Jeremiah 31:3 (New Life Version)

I am not a chef and that was pretty evident in the workings of my kitchen yesterday.

I found out my knives could be sharper and yet they were sharp enough to insert themselves into my skin.

Ouch!

Even though I technically do not know how to fillet anything I did a number on my finger.

So I had to pause.

I was on a mission to whip up this meal and so I didn't want to have to pause.

I really never want to pause. It doesn't come naturally and when it's required I fight it even more.

The amazing T-Squad came to the Band-Aid rescue and I went back to try to work on the meal.

I wasn't so successful as the finger would not stop throbbing and bleeding.

I sent out an SOS to a super friend.

She showed up and informed me I would need to pause, aka 'sit down' and apply pressure to get it to stop bleeding.

My friend knows me.

She knew what she was asking and I guess she was willing to risk our friendship over this.

I sat down on a bar stool in my kitchen and applied pressure for about a minute.

Applying pressure hurt so I peeked under the gauze and it was still bleeding.

My friend gave me the *'really Nichole?'* look.

The look that meant I was not being patient and that I would have to sit there and really give it time to stop bleeding - the first step in healing.

Applying pressure hurt.

Oh boy, it was as if Jesus put up a big white screen in my kitchen and played some pretty amazing scenes of my life.

I was watching scenes played back of times that I haven't taken the time to heal.

Why?

All because I didn't want to pause.

Didn't want to sit.

I wasn't willing to take the time.

Knowing that applying pressure would hurt.

Focusing on the 'owie' hurt.

It would be much easier to find a distraction and just keep going. But my friend… she had the love and patience of Jesus. Eventually it quit bleeding. On went a new Band-Aid and the healing would continue.

We meditated on Your unfailing love. For this God is our God for ever and ever; he will be our guide even to the end. Psalm 48:9b, 14

This morning I'm typing with nine fingers, my right pointer finger is still sore and bandaged. I am thankful, thankful that there is a process to healing. I am thankful for love being patient and never failing!

'Constant through the trial and the change
One thing remains
Your love never fails it never gives up it never runs out on me.'[2]

Give me a course and I will follow it, for the most part! I had the honor and privilege of running Hood to Coast last weekend. Hood to Coast is a team relay running race. It starts at Mount Hood and finishes on the Oregon Coast. I knew each time I was to get out of the van what was expected of me. Run. Funny that as I am typing I can hear God speaking over this… "Nichole you only knew a portion of what Hood to Coast was going to be. You knew how to run. But you didn't know the climate, the scenery, the 'issues' (lack of sleep, diarrhea, not eating regularly), that would come up. You didn't know the exact times of the day. You just knew you were going on a journey." True, but I know how to run. So each time I could get out of the van and do that. I could run.

It hit me, writing this book has been a journey. A journey I never 'wanted' to go on. Running in Hood to Coast was something I always dreamed of doing. Is God comparing this book writing process to a journey? It could totally compare. I for sure don't know all the details! How long is the book? When is it going to be done? And the major one I struggle with each time, I DON'T KNOW HOW TO WRITE! God asks me, "Nichole why are you still hung up on that detail?" Well let's see God, maybe because to write a book you should be a writer and I don't feel like one. It's easier to run when you 'feel' like you can do it. He asks me again, "Do you remember Hood to Coast? Did you always feel 'ready to run' or like you could do it? Did you experience some of the same emotions and feelings? Did you have any anxiety, worry about other's expectations of you? Were you tired? Unsure of the exact course? Having to do something when your body felt icky? Nichole focus on Me, remember the reason for this. Remember your purpose. Remember why I do all things for you. I love you Nichole."

On Saturday we gathered as a family to scatter my grandma and grandpa's ashes under the tree on their property. God was there. I became even more aware of God's love for me. He was in the tears, the prayers, the walking around the property. He brought comfort to my earthly loss. As I am walking around my grandparent's property I realize God has planned every situation on purpose for me. He is The Author of my life story. I re-read that last sentence. I am NOT the writer, He is! I need to stay focused on this, He is writing through me.

I am also being made aware that I am not to just write and talk about love and grace but that I am to live in them daily, in ALL my relationships.

My Prayer: Thank You Lord for the past, the present and the future. Knowing You were in it, are in it and will be in it, brings peace and comfort to me. Thank You Lord for lessons learned. Thank You for Your amazing patience with me. Thank You for Your constant provision. Sometimes thinking about my history and where I have been and what I have done brings a sadness and confusion of how and why You would stay with me and bring me to this point. Then, in this moment when I stop and pause to truly let in sink in, it's You, it's all Your amazing love. You have a purpose, a purpose to pursue Your people. Oh Lord even me, a girl who has sinned, who has fallen, who has said the wrong things, who has doubted, who has questioned, who has made stubborn silly choices, You love me. Lord may this journey with You be all about me desiring to know You more. May it really be about stripping off that which hinders me from becoming the girl You created me to be. May my hand hold tight to Your's. Knowing and trusting that You will lead in Your perfect way and time. May I find You in the everyday moments. May I not stay here in my brokenness. I need grace and love to fill my voids, may I stay out of the way. May I keep my mind and heart aware that I need to be loved on by You, not because I deserve it or can earn it, but rather because of who You are, You are love. May I be willing to travel this journey in Your timing, even when the pain of each step makes me want to run. May I know that true healing is in Your hands. Following me with Your Love has included an amazing husband, my boys, family and friends, and in the everyday life moments with people. May I become more aware of Your Love for me in Your Word. Amen.

Obedience

Lately I have been thinking about how I just want to complete this book, get it done and move on. Do what you asked me to do. Go on to the next thing. Like its holding me back from other stuff. Just now in the shower I felt grief over that. Who am I to think that I am in control of this process? Yet I always try to be! Even though this book writing process has been some of the hardest years of my life, I am grateful for this journey. Who am I to rush this process? Who am I to want it to be over? Yet I feel pressure to finish. What if I don't get this book done before Jesus comes back? There are many unknowns with this book writing process and not being in control and that is way outside of my comfort zone.

The end of a matter is better than its beginning, and
patience is better than pride. Ecclesiastes 7:8

I know it's not my timing; I am not in control. I am to trust and obey.

Note from my Bible on Ecclesiastes 7:8: "To finish what we start takes hard work, wise guidance, self-discipline, and patience. Anyone with vision can start a big project. But vision without wisdom often results in unfinished projects and goals."

I am so easily distracted by the sound of the phone signaling I have a text from the Engineer, and when I look at the text I see I have an email… oooh from JCPenney offering me 20% off my next order. The dryer will let me know soon when the towels are dry. I am easily distracted.

I have been working on this book for years! This morning I feel like I have failed Him. To be perfectly honest I know I have avoided it, tried to wish it away and at times make it go away. Through flat out avoidance and some not so creative distraction methods I have not been obedient. I can come up with many 'excuses'. I do things well that I know I can do well. I can do something that has a time frame because I know a beginning and an ending. It would be so GREAT if God could flash a date that He wanted the book completed by across my screen right - now that would be so awesome. I would make that happen.

I hear Him… "Daughter, you are seeing this all wrong. Your focus is off. You are seeing this as a to-do. It's not a to-do. This is your journey. Our relationship. This is about Me and what I have for you. This is about you knowing you are loved. How am I supposed to put a time frame on that? For you need to experience Me. You need to spend time with Me. This is not a start and finish type of thing. The book is Mine, let me do that. You just be in My love."

My heart is racing right now. For again it's about me choosing to be obedient to something I can't control. I am not in control. I just don't want to let Him down. I want to do it right. What if I wasted too much time?

"Nichole why spend time thinking about what was, and what you could have done different? Why not be in this moment with Me? Why are you choosing to avoid this moment?"

Because I am still not sure I deserve this moment. This moment of freedom and grace! This moment of the most amazing pouring down of love. How can this moment be if I didn't get it right? If I didn't earn it, how come this moment is here? What if I come to accept this moment and then in my humanness mess it up worrying? I am human.

"Yeah I am fully aware. I created you. I know you and I love you."

Why do I think I know myself better than He does? Is it because I can't let go of past mistakes or future possibilities of mistakes? I need to fully 100% submit to the fact that I am not in control. I don't need to just write about it, or blog about it, or FB status about it, or tell my friends and family about it. I NEED to live it. I need to live each moment submitted to Him. It needs to be the one constant in my life and from that everything else will be balanced.

To God's elect, who have been chosen according to the foreknowledge of God the Father, through the sanctifying work of the Spirit, to be obedient to Jesus Christ and sprinkled by His blood: Grace and peace be yours in abundance. 1 Peter 1:1

I am having a hard time 'feeling' like God's elect this morning. Rather I 'feel' more like a hot mess of emotions. God purposefully chose me, chose me to be in relationship with Him. In a relationship in which He would sanctify (set me apart). Not me figuring it out, or getting my act together, but God working on me.

Grace and peace be yours in abundance. 1 Peter 1:2

This is what I need. Grace to live and breathe, and peace to be still.

Who through faith are shielded by God's power. 1 Peter 1:5

God is protecting me. Even though I feel like the enemy has cornered me and has blasted me until I can't see and breathe, God is protecting me. This is where I have to choose to live on faith and not my feelings.

Though now for a little while you may have had to suffer grief in all kinds of trials. 1 Peter 1:6

Trials not to break me, but to build me strong. Trying to remember that any trial I go through or experience will be very insignificant in comparison to the cross. I can't claim to follow after Jesus and not embrace suffering and tribulation. Jesus said it would happen. (Mark 8:34-38)

These (trials) have come so that your faith - of greater worth than gold, which perishes even though refined by fire - may be proved genuine and may result in praise, glory and honor when Jesus Christ is revealed. 1 Peter 1:7

Refinement in the fire is hot and it burns. It burns hot. Not focusing on the process but looking forward to the finished product is choosing faith and not feelings.

Though you have not seen Him, you love Him; and even though you do not see Him now, you believe in Him and are filled with an inexpressible and glorious joy, for you are receiving the goal of your faith, the salvation of your souls. 1 Peter 1:8-9

Here is the instruction of how to live today;

Be Holy 1 Peter 1:13-25

Therefore, prepare your minds for action; be self-controlled; set your hope fully on the grace to be given you when Jesus Christ is revealed. As obedient children, do not conform to the evil desire you had when you lived in ignorance. But just as He who called you is holy, so be holy in all you do; for it is written: "Be holy, because I am holy." Since you call on a Father who judges each man's work impartially, live your lives as strangers here in reverent fear. For you know that it was not with perishable things such as silver or gold that you were redeemed from the empty way of life handed down to you from your forefathers, but with the precious blood of Christ, a lamb without blemish or defect. He was chosen before the creation of the world, but was revealed in these last times for your sake. Through Him you believe in God, who raised Him from the dead and glorified Him, and so your faith and hope are in God.

Now that you have purified yourselves by obeying the truth so that you have sincere love for your brothers, love one another deeply, from the heart. For you have been born again, not of perishable seed, but of imperishable, through the living and enduring word of God. For, all men are like grass, and all their glory is like the flowers of the field; the grass withers and the flowers fade, but the Word of the Lord stands forever. And this is the Word that was preached to you.

There were three opportunities this weekend to practice my reactions to situations, to try the whole self-control thing.

- I did not react well.
- I was easily angered and frustrated.
- I did not choose compassion, love and grace.
- I am mad at myself.

Now, as I sit here early this morning I have a choice to make.

I can choose to live on in my feelings of disappointment with myself.

OR

I can choose to hear what Jesus is speaking to my heart.

He knew each of these situations.

He knew the timing.

He knew my reactions.

I can choose to learn the lesson.

A lesson in choosing faith over feelings.

I choose to apply grace to this weekend.

I choose to know that self-disappointment, pouting, wallowing in yuck will NOT redeem my bad first reactions.

Choosing to believe His way works, despite the way I feel.

Feelings are not dictators. Feelings are just that, feelings, they should not be given free reign and complete control.

As I read Ezekiel 20 this morning I am reminded of just how loving, persistent, faithful, and amazing God is. During my times of rebellion, stubbornness, and sin He still loves me. He still desires to be with me.

I am reading about the Israelites this morning and I am reminded about the journey I am on. That sometimes my choices and decisions, have led me farther from Him. It breaks me this morning, as I know it breaks His heart. As I walk with Him I hope I will learn quicker. I hope to learn to sense when I am walking away due to pride, stubbornness, and selfishness. For He remains constant. He disciplines because He loves me. I know that God is good, (Psalm 135) and so everything He does is good. This journey has been hard. God has purpose in everything He does. The journey was hard on purpose so that I would feel needy and weak and come to rely and depend on Him and not myself.

*Here's what will happen. While you're out among the nations where God has dispersed you and the blessings and curses come in just the way I have set them before you, and you and your children take them seriously and come back to God, your God, and **obey** him with your whole heart and soul according to everything that I command you today, God, your God, will restore everything you lost; he'll have compassion on you; he'll come back and pick up the pieces from all the places where you were scattered.*
*I call Heaven and Earth to witness against you today: I place before you Life and Death, Blessing and Curse. Choose life so that you and your children will live. And love God, your God, listening **obediently** to him, firmly embracing him. Oh yes, he is life itself, a long life settled on the soil that God, your God, promised to give your ancestors, Abraham, Isaac, and Jacob. Deuteronomy 30:1-4, 19-20 (The Message - emphasis mine)*

Recently I was approached and asked to join a team.

In the hours since being asked, I have truly wrestled it out with God.

My head hurts. My body is tired.

I feel like I have lost. Lost the battle of the will.

I gave Him the, "I really don't want to do this" line so many times over the past 48 hours.

My 'I don't want to' came, backed up with many reasons.

I fought Him on location. I fought Him on the price tag attached. I fought Him on who I would be working with. I fought Him on who I would be serving. I fought Him on what it would keep me from. I fought Him on how much time it could take. I fought Him on the purpose of all of it.

In the last hours of the fight I yelled at Him, "Prove me wrong then". Not a proud moment. But I am being honest.

I am truly tired from this fight.

I hear a very calm and patient voice say,

"I want to humble you. I want to teach you. I want you to know you can obey with a good attitude. I want you to be stretched. I want to remove more pride. I want to show you love."

A few of those sound great, but I have to admit there are a few things there that I would rather not be involved with. Feeling like a girly who just gave it her all to 'get out of this' I grab tight to my Jesus' hand and trust He knows better.

I am still scared. TERRIFIED. Still wanting Him to prove my flesh wrong. Expecting Him to show up big.

Doing the will of God from your heart. Ephesians 6:6b

Obedience comes from the heart. Where love resides.

Obedience. The Bible teaches that if I love God I will obey Him. I can think of many times I chose not to obey. I didn't obey because it felt too overwhelming to do it His way. Or I didn't obey because I was afraid, or I didn't trust. I didn't obey because I was worried what others would think or say about me. I didn't obey because I thought my way was better.

He learned obedience from what He suffered. Hebrews 5:8

Obedience doesn't come naturally. Rather it is a learned behavior. It is a following of what is expected, an understanding of consequences an acknowledgment of guidelines.

What am I suffering?

My own pride, selfishness, stubbornness. I am suffering because of lack of complete submission.

He learned obedience from what He suffered. Hebrews 5:8

He being Jesus. Of course He was God's Son, but He came to fully submit Himself as a human. Why? For His benefit of experiencing life here on earth? I don't think so. His obedience came because He fully submitted to the will His Father had for Him. And it didn't look all pretty, clean, and fun. Jesus' obedience led Him to the cross and it cost Him His life. Jesus' obedience displayed pure and perfect love.

Being asked to obey won't always be easy, fun, or even make sense.

Walk in obedience to all that the Lord your God has commanded
you, so that you may live and prosper and prolong your days
in the land that you will possess. Deuteronomy 5:33

However there is a healthy balance that needs to be obtained here. A balance of His unconditional love and my obedience. Not my earning, achieving or striving.

'Trust and obey for there's no other way.'[1]

My heart hears:

"My ways are not your ways Nichole. Trust and obey. Do what I have asked you to do. And know that I will take care of you. I have never let you down."

But if anyone obeys His word, God's love is truly
made complete in him. 1 John 2:5

And my heart hears;

"I've asked you to love the people, serve the people, bring smiles and joy, get to know them, listen to them."

I am reminded it's not about the church, the Café team or coffee drinks; it's about the people.

I am not writing you a new command but one we have had from
the beginning. I ask that we love one another. And this is love: that
we walk in obedience to his commands. As you have heard from the
beginning, his command is that you walk in love. 2 John 5-6

My Prayer: An obedience that didn't look or sound so pretty many times. Which makes me stand back in awe that God can work through my feeble attempt at obedience. From obedience I learned that respect, patience, love, endurance, perseverance, commitment, and submission will be woven in at just the right times. I fell down quite a few times, with the skinned knees came tears, pride removal, honesty, and obedience. Thank You for each one of these times. Thank You for not taking me out of any of the circumstances of this past year. Thank You for holding my hand, wiping my tears, and whispering to my heart, "there is purpose even in this." Amen.

Walking on Sunshine

I had one of 'those Sundays' yesterday. Now if you are male and reading this, this might go right past you so fast you can't even see it, but if you are female, oh boy am I hoping there is another female out there on planet earth that has had one of 'those Sundays'. Oh and just so you know, I have had SO many of them, that's why they are officially called 'those Sundays'.

I woke up in a GREAT mood, ready to start the day, I went in and greeted the boys and told them good morning and they were both so excited that its 'SNACK Sunday' (what the T-Squad calls Super Bowl Sunday), the day where there is a table full of snacks and they get to pick whatever they want! The morning was going just dandy until I walked into the kitchen. I was hit with the thought all of a sudden of being the only female in this house, now it's something I live with everyday so I'm really not exactly sure why it's bothering this particular morning? From that moment on it was like my brain had an extra surge of hormones and emotions and all my thoughts were out of whack. Everything was disturbing me, from too many cracker boxes being opened in the pantry, to being called out to look at some 'spots' on someone's head, to sitting at the table surrounded by boys all excited about the 'snacks' and all I could 'feel' was lonely, oh and a little overwhelmed at the thought of having to make all the snacks.

After breakfast I headed off to get dressed and get ready for church. I was standing in my closet having one of the infamous battles of what to wear. There was nothing to wear. The tears were pouring out. The emotions were at an all-time high. At one point the amazing Engineer entered the closest to 'help' with the outfit. Friends, it didn't go so well for him, the closest is small and the hormones were too large!

I eventually found something to wear, which unfortunately did not make me 'feel' any better. But at least I was clothed and ready to go out in public.

Praying and hoping that 'church' will solve my mental frame of mind.

I delivered the youngest of the T-Squad to his class. I was greeted by the teacher. She greeted me and reminded me that I haven't served time - oops I mean volunteered in the classroom lately. She told me that I needed to *pick a place to serve because I wasn't serving in the church*. What?! This was MORE than my little mind and heart could take. All of me wanted to leave that church and never come back in. I wanted to go back to my closet, sit on the floor in my jammie pants with a 9x13 pan of brownies and just cry. However being that I am a girlie, who has stepped out and is trying this whole obedience and self-control thing, there are no brownies, just tears!

I immediately went to hating the church. It totally messed with me and flustered me. Didn't anyone notice or see I was listening to God? I am being obedient. I am serving where He has asked me to serve. In my home, taking care of The Engineer and the T-Squad. When I walked into the worship service all my flesh could see and hear was a room full of hypocrites. Sunday morning actors and actresses, people who were going through the motions. I was judging them. I hated the church, I hated being there and I wanted nothing to do with it. When The Engineer saw me he knew I was not at peace. I have always been so discreet with my emotions. HA!

I informed The Engineer of what had just went down and he kept repeating, "don't let it bother you, don't let it get to you." How in the world could I do that? Easy for the calm, collected, non-hormonal Engineer to spout off. I cried, "God if You want me to stay in this church then I need You to tell me what to do." I got up and went and found a calm, collected female friend and told her everything. All the yucky things I was thinking and feeling. She listened and then very boldly stated, "You get your marching orders from God alone and NO ONE else!" She told me to hold my head up in confidence in God and go back out there and be the wife and mom my family needed me to be.

I get my marching orders from God and God alone
(2 Timothy 2:3-4, Joshua 1:1-18 The Message)

I made it through the worship service and came back home. I was in that closet of mine, I was changing clothes and asking "Why in the world did today bother me so bad?" and boy did God answer;

"Because you still care about what others think of you, you want and need their approval with all of this."

Hi, I am Nichole and I am a people pleaser. I am including this little section here in the book to hopefully find other people like me or better yet, for you to try and understand people like me!

In these most recent weeks I have found myself called out by other people on choices I have made, things I have said, or stuff I did. I will be honest, my first reaction was to make it 'all okay' with them and get them to like me and do it fast. If you are a people pleaser you know that feeling of having someone not quite like you, well it's just unsettling and makes life feel more like, 'walking on egg shells' than 'walking on sunshine'.

I am a girlie who does life better while 'walking on sunshine'. I know life is not all about happy cheery sunny rainbows but when you are a people pleaser you find yourself trying to create that world. Constantly. You find yourself in a very unhealthy cycle.

*Am I now trying to win the approval of men, or of God? Or
am I trying to please men? If I were still trying to please men,
I would not be a servant of Christ. Galatians 1:10*

In these most recent weeks instead of tethered and chained to that
unhealthy cycle, I have rather found myself before my Creator learning, desiring and wanting to do it His way. Now that is no doing of my
own. I can't even say I know how to position myself properly; sometimes I just end up falling down on my face.

If you are people pleaser you will be able to relate to that 'pressur-
ing feeling'. We have to make it right, we have to make them like us
again; we have to get back to walking on sunshine!

"Keep your face always toward the sunshine - and shadows will fall behind you."[1]

I need to take every situation before God and allow Him to speak
words of truth to me. Because I know there have been times that I have
made a wrong move, said a wrong word, and I have had to go back
and make it right. That's not people pleasing, that's asking for forgiveness - and God help me not to mix up the two.

*Blessed are those who have learned to acclaim you, who walk
in the light of your presence, O LORD. Psalm 89:15*

My Prayer: You are my sunshine. May my eyes be fixed on You.
I answer to You and You alone. I was not created to people please.
I was created to be loved and to love. Amen.

My Own Walk – Others Have Theirs

This insanely weird visual just popped into my blonde little head. So what if you could walk into this big ole warehouse and 'shop' for the life you wanted. This is so crazy, but think about it. Walk down each isle and pick out the body, the hairstyle and color, the skin tone, personality. Wouldn't this be amazing? How many of us already spend time doing this anyway? I know I have. I have spent too many minutes wanting and desiring that which I don't have. Because anything but what I currently have would be better. Right? Wouldn't life be better if I had her job? Her hair? Her body? I wish I didn't have to admit this, but it's true. I have been judgmental, envious, jealous and focused on others and their lives!

What do judgment, comparison, jealousy, and envy have in common?

Judgment is to form an opinion of **another**. Comparison is to examine **another** in order to observe differences or similarities. Jealousy is a feeling of resentment against **another** because of something they have. Envy is a feeling of discontent in regard to **another** who appears to have advantages.

Judgment, comparison, jealousy and envy need our focus, energy and attention on how we measure up to each other. Are we better or worse, more or less? It's a constant internal dialogue that goes on.

I have so many examples unfortunately, in which I have focused on another. Another momma. Another wife. Another writer. Another runner.

I have found myself in the middle of running a race and instead of focusing on breathing, or pacing myself, I am checking out how fast the other runners are running. Who is ahead of me? Who am I going to beat across the finish line?

"It's very hard in the beginning to understand that the whole idea is not to beat the other runners. Eventually you learn that the competition is against the little voice inside you that wants you to quit."[1]

I have my own walk and others have theirs.

Let's just go ahead and be what we were made to be, without enviously or pridefully comparing ourselves with each other, or trying to be something we aren't. Romans 12:5 (The Message)

When we first moved to Washington I remember wanting and needing a friend who would be in the same season of life as me and who would bring out the best in my original design. Not just a 'yes' girl. I wanted someone who was willing to do the hard parts of life with me. I prayed for such a friend. God answered. He gave me a woman who was full of life, energy, and laughter. He gave me a woman who was truthful, sometimes to a fault! We would stand on the corner right next to the school after we shared our boys with their teachers for the day and have some hard conversations. When one of us needed cheering on, the other one lifted the pom-poms. When one of us needed steering the other one did the correcting. Mind you all of this was done from hearts filled with Jesus' love. There were so many amazing moments of investment into my soul at her kitchen table. This wasn't always an easy friendship; we worked hard to stay connected at the heart. When needed, we took breaks, asked for forgiveness and built back anything we had lost in each other.

One morning in particular, I was lamenting on how so and so felt about me, and what would they think about me? When with great courage my friend boldly said, "You are worried everyone will judge you because that's how you treat them." As these words came in and landed on my heart, they stung. I knew within seconds of hearing them that there was truth in them and that God wanted me to hear them.

We tend to notice in others that which resides in us.

I am very critical of self. I was judging myself on performance, and I was judging others on the same scale. I was treating others how I treated myself - but not in the 'right' way.

One morning as I was returning from walking the boys to school when I heard God say to me, "Nichole, don't be so quick to judge and hard on others. Because you hold yourself to such a standard it doesn't mean I do, nor do I of others. I love simply you and simply them! I don't require anything for My love. I don't need anything from you to love you. I just love!"

My job is NOT to work things out in others, but to do life with them.

I am very aware of the sin and yuck that still exists in me. The thoughts that are judgmental and critical. I am judging others because I judge myself.

Being stripped of that which keeps us from living in our original design is painful. It hurts to have it removed. I lived for years thinking God was judging me, which meant I needed to be very critical of myself. Unfortunately I passed judgment onto those around me. If I was living with a certain standard or expectation of myself, then I held those around me to the same standard.

MY OWN WALK - OTHERS HAVE THEIRS

Be completely humble and gentle, be patient, bearing
with one another in love. Ephesians 4:2

Why am I so easily unsettled and bothered in the church? Why am I irritated about all the inclusiveness inside the doors and how it feels the church is exclusive; wanting to keep 'those people' who are not rule followers out? Why? I think I am most critical of people who I think should know better. The church people! Why have I NOT offered grace, love and patience with the people inside the church? Why was I 'thinking, assuming and saying they should know better'? How in the world did I decide I was any better?

Why can't I just love them?

God will work with others and it's NONE of my business.

Who am I to worry or judge another's path, journey, and choices? I need to mind my own business. I am so not perfect and for me to have the expectation that others will be, is so ridiculous.

My own walk - others have theirs.

Beyond all these things put on love, which is the perfect bond of
unity. Colossians 3:14 (New American Standard Bible)

I am at the tire shop while they put new tires on my Subaru Outback. I am trying to work on the book, to put things in order so they flow. Yesterday The Engineer informed me he would like to write a book. You wanna guess where I was sitting when he said that? I was soaking in the sun on our back porch. The words just seemed to come out of him with excitement. Like he really wanted to do it. I was a little jealous, okay more like insanely jealous. I know The Engineer will be able to write a most amazing book. He will be able to create chapters, and flow, and complete sentences. I might just end up with a bunch of thoughts/ideas/words saved into my laptop. But I pause and take a deep breath right here in the middle of this tire smelling building and remember I am to be obedient to what God is asking of me. Focus on my own path.

My own walk - others have theirs.

There is freedom in focus. Focus on what is right within your view. To be aware of what you have, what you need. To not lose focus, nor drift on to the path or journey of another. This is not selfishness or the lack of empathy, but rather the self-control to not be judgmental or jealous. What is everyone else doing? Eating fad diets, over scheduling themselves, running hard to avoid the peace and calm that the soul desires. Why? Why do we do it? We do, we fight against that which comes natural, that for which we were created. To live at peace. To be content. Is it because we think we will fulfill those very things we were created to need? Created to need - how hard that is to say, to type out. It seems so desperate. So lacking. So needy and yet coming to terms with our need. The depth of our need. Knowing that it doesn't go further than our Creator can fulfill. Need versus want.

I fought and argued with God when I was invited to join the café team at church. I didn't want to be fighting Him, or be disobedient, or dodging. I want to do what He asked me to do. I wanted to be obedient. I struggle, why?

"Because you don't believe in Me. You believe in the power of you, which is nothing and amounts to nothing but stubborn pride. Nichole I need and want you to believe in Me. Trust Me. Trust that I love you. Allow Me to fully love you. Please Nichole."

With that big pep talk from my Creator I boldly step forth in obedience and join the café team. It was very difficult for me to be very loving to the church people because I was assuming they 'knew better'. That they should be behaving like God loved them. But it just dawned on me that maybe they didn't know. Just like I didn't know for the longest time. I didn't really **know** God loved me. I didn't **know** it in my heart. I never sat still and quieted myself long enough to hear it. How many more are running? Busying themselves? How many are trying to hide? To drown out God? Out of shame, guilt, and fear?! Not thinking they are deserving. The people on the other side of the church doors are not healthier. Nope we are just in a building. A building that means nothing unless we know God loves us. For it's not location that saves us. It's not a denomination. It's not a Bible study, tithing, choir practice. It's none of the events or things. It's only Him. God pursues us. He saves us. God heals us. All because He loves us.

My Prayer: Thank You for being in control so I can 'learn' I don't have to. Lord help me to keep my eyes off everyone else, it is NOT my business how they are doing their ministry, how they are living their life. Father, forgive me for my judgment attitude. Forgive me for not extending Your love to all Your people. I am not to change people. I pray for patience and mercy with others. Help me to not be judgmental of others and their journey. I pray for the grace and love to look and see others the way You see them. Whether I was angry, bitter, or confused, thank You for showing me my errors. I realize tonight that this was part of the journey. All of it. Everything You knew. None of it surprises You. Thank You for pursing me and loving me enough to keep teaching me this. Thank You for loving me as if there was no other option. For right now You are smiling on me. You love me. You adore me. Out of that contented, peace and joy filled whole life I will live. I will breathe. I will do life. Help me to continue to follow You and Your Way. Help me to seek You with my whole mind, heart and soul. Help me to not settle for this season of life and get comfortable here. But help me to know You more each and every day. Thank You for every detail that Your hand creates. Each intimate personal detail for me. Will You help me to continue to grow in love? Your perfect love. Help me to know this love is what went before me. You love also stays with me. It surrounds me. Your love. Amen.

One Thing Remains

I am being reminded this morning that the enemy will stop at nothing.

He is nasty and fights nasty.

He is killing our joy.

He is stealing our peace.

He is destroying everything he can get his hands on.

Marriages, families, relationships, people.

But it's time we acknowledge this. Truly call him on it.

Trying to figure out why things are not good.

Whining that our bodies our limiting our capabilities right now to exercise so we are not able to go out and run. (Okay maybe that one is just personal to me.)

Worrying about things we have no control over.

We need to STOP.

We need to realize the enemy does a stinking celebration dance and grins from ear to disgusting ear every time he distracts us.

The thief comes only to steal and kill and destroy, John 10:10a

His job is to be nasty, every single time.

There is NO good in him. None. Zilch. Nada.

We need to call him on this, because he will stop at nothing to keep us from what we were created for.

Finish reading John 10:10...

I have come that they may have life, and have it to the full.

That's our Jesus speaking. He came so that we could have joy, peace, security, faith and, love.

Call the enemy on what he is doing...

Then focus completely on Jesus, grab His hand and walk this day with your head help up knowing that you were created to live in love. His love!

Know that God will stop at nothing too!

I have pushed back at God. I have not always trusted Him. I have strayed and doubted. My heart still questions "Why?", "How come?"

Even as I am fully known. 1 Corinthians 13:12b

God knows me.

It seems simple and complex all swirled together. Kind of like those ice cream cones that you can get where the chocolate and vanilla are swirled together. I want to be the plain purified clean white vanilla, (**and to The Engineer and T-squad vanilla is a flavor) but the brown, smudgy, not so put together and imperfect chocolate is mixed right close.

He knows me and He doesn't refuse to come in close. To hold me, to love me for me. My thoughts, words, actions and all. God loves all of me - all of my swirled together self.

I am prepping for a busy week, making lists, lists of what needs to be done, writing a grocery list. I am weeding the yard, scrubbing toilets, cleaning floors, doing laundry and feeding the dog. I am trying to be a momma to two energy filled boys, making meals, remembering to brush my teeth, trying to get enough sleep, trying not to procrastinate, prepping for the oldest little guy's birthday, trying not to forget back to school is just around the corner. I'm also checking the mail, which leads to stress when envelopes get opened and bills appear from out of nowhere. Thinking about whether my eyebrows need to be tamed, still working on being the supportive, loving submissive Engineer's wife.

Taking a deep breath I read:

> *For I am convinced that neither death nor life, neither angels nor demons, neither the present nor the future, nor any powers, neither height nor depth, nor anything else in all creation, will be able to separate us from the love of God that is in Christ Jesus our Lord. Romans 8:38-39*

So the cliff note of that verse is;
For what we go through in this world cannot separate us from the love of God.

Nothing can.

Not hormones.

Not our own agenda.

Not our sleep deprived minds.

Not our dogs, toilets, weeds in our yard.

Not our lack of parenting skills.

Not our bills, money, and credit cards.

Not even our out of control eyebrows!

In his book, *The Power of a Whisper. Hearing God. Having the guts to respond.*[1] Bill Hybels refers to Romans 8:38-39;

"For most people, it's an utterly overwhelming idea that a loving and all-powerful God wants to share an intimate bond with the likes of you or me - but this passage assures us that He does. Through one simple verse of Scripture, God seems to remind us, 'I know you're going to foul up. I'll forgive you. I know you're going to get scared as well, and I promise to help you with that. You won't always pray as wisely as you hope, but I promise that Holy Spirit will give expression to what you don't even realize you ought to be praying. Just keep your hand in mine, and we'll walk together each step of the way. I'll cover you. I'll love you. I'll never leave you. I'll always be your God.'"

In Spite Of.

Three words given to me a few days ago.

I knew at the time these words would have some big purpose and meaning.

If there is one thing I am good at that also can be a huge fault of mine, is that I am emotional.

I live life with tons of emotion.

I experience pure uninterrupted joy and I experience heartache and devastating pain. This pendulum of emotion can swing from one end to the other all within a New York minute!

In this season Team Hamblin has a lot going on. We are surrounded with some unknowns. Public school some days is a battlefield for two young boys. There is this book that needs writing. Oh and we live in a country that is in a bit of a whirlwind because of the newest political statistics, but I can't let my emotions dictate the course of my life.

I repeat, I cannot allow my emotions to lead.

No, rather in spite of how I feel, or what I think, I need to remain on course.

I need to remember who I get my marching orders from.

I need to remember my purpose.

For that has not changed.

In spite of unknowns that come with life I am to remain in His love for me.

Remaining there will be what brings peace, contentment and joy.

In spite of how I feel.

I am to remain in Love.

You see I have learned my emotions are not always reliable they can change!

But He won't.

He is constant.

He is reliable.

He is love.

Love.
The One Thing that Remains.

It is 11:12a.m and I am working on notes and stuff (love that all-inclusive word.) and for probably the first time I am aware of how at peace I am. Truly at peace knowing that I am right where God wants me. I am loved. I don't feel rushed, panicky, or afraid. I feel at peace right here right now knowing that the process of writing this book is not about the finished book (thank God for teaching me this!). For in the beginning I was stressed about writing a book, worried, doubting, fearing the book. Worried I had wasted time, worried I would never finish, worried I couldn't write. This book was an amazing gift to me. Each word. Each sentence. To teach me that God loves me. He loves me! What a journey this book writing has been.

My Prayer: Dear Jesus will You remind me today that 'in spite of' all that surrounds me, good or bad You are in control? You see me and also this world I live in. I am Yours. You love me. Help me to know this. Lord, please help me to remain in Your love. I pray against the swirl of busy thoughts. Help me to focus on the moment I am in. Help me to remain here with You, with Your face shining upon me. Amen.

Self-Control

The older I get the more I have learned (boy do I remember SO disliking when others, 'older others' would say that phrase) but really life experiences bring lessons to be learned. Wisdom comes upon us when we allow those life experiences to teach us something.

I am choosing to write this morning while the boys are at baseball camp. In all honesty my humanness would rather be out shopping. Which is so weird to me because I thought I had reigned in the whole 'run' thing. But as I sit here this morning at my laptop I am realizing this will always be a struggle. A struggle that proves my dependency on my Creator. To stay within my balanced boundaries. Boundaries that provide me with genuine enduring love, a peace and comfort that calms.

I wake some days thinking I know I am to submit and follow the Lord's agenda for the day. And there are other days where I feel very sure that I have the correct 'to do' list. Monday was such a hard and overwhelming day for me. I had a headache and belly ache. All I could do was lay on the couch and rest. My mind swirled with a dialogue of what I needed to be doing, or should be doing. I was feeling guilty. That resting was a waste of my Creator's time. I know it's the same rock that I have circled in this wilderness before. It is Wednesday morning and I am here because I am seeking peace. I am seeking God. I am thankful He brings me to awareness of His presence. For without God I cannot see or hear. I am fully dependent on Him. Each and every breath I take. I feel like a student who is packed full of great information and lessons that my Creator has taught me, but like a school girl walking down the hall of life I can't seem to 'balance' all that I am learning. I easily get overwhelmed. I doubt if I am truly hearing correctly and if I am capable to apply these lessons.

I have now learned that there is peace and contentment here at the laptop. Writing is becoming a place of refuge; which makes me nervous as I type. Why? Is it because I might just get down to the real honesty of my own soul? A place I am not truly aware of. It's easy to write about things we know. But what about what we don't know. And why is it that there are things about ourselves that we don't know? For me, I have been with myself for 36 years and counting so how could there be things I don't know? Time being still. Taking the time to find and see what is there. I can't dwell on the thought of all the things I have missed on the way. It saddens my heart to think of things I didn't see, hear, or experience because I rushed and pushed past them so quickly.

There was a time when I so badly, didn't want to write this book. That time quickly bled over into the time of just wanting to hurry up and write it. If I get it done I can move on to 'other' things. I can still sense in my flesh the want and need to busy myself with other things. To distract myself, which I have learned is my way of avoiding a revelation, a lesson or a healing moment with my Creator. As I type I want to share my heart, knowing that when it comes through my fingertips onto this screen before me I will truly be able to breathe deeper. Deeper into the places that have been cleared and readied for Him.

I desperately want to keep 'writing' chapters in the book, but as I flip over to that file nothing is coming right now. So I wait and trust in His timing. I refuse to allow the enemy to capture me with his lies. He is lying to me. Lying and saying that I am 'not a writer' and that I will never get this 'right'. Lord I am choosing to hear You right now…

"It's more than the book. It's not about getting it right. It's about time with me. You and Me together. Allowing Me to love on you. So

Nichole be strong and don't allow the enemy to tarnish that with his lies. I love you Nichole."

Some days I must admit my awareness is not there. For my thoughts get stuck on self. Whether it is a method of distraction or my allowance of worry and doubt to crowd out the calm peaceful place of my Jesus.

Over and over the message is about me not being in control and how the desire and urge has to be broken in me.

I have an intense headache that has been this way now for about two weeks. Today, as I am waiting in the room to see the doctor, is a great time to have a big conversation with God.

I yell out, "I know I am not in control. I got it now! Can we move on?"

To which He boldly, lovingly and gracefully responds;

"Do you really get it?"

"Yes. I know I am not in control. You are. I am so not in control. I can't drive myself, I can't take care of my family, I can't even write!"

And then I added in this,

"You know the book You asked me to write, WHAT IF I CAN'T FINISH IT? It just proves I am a failure and I have nothing to offer and I am not good. I can't even be obedient with this."

The room is bright, sterile, cold and I am sitting here in pain and God responds;

"What if? What if you don't finish the book? What if you can't write? I don't need anything from you. I didn't ask you to write the book for Me. It was for you. For you to know I love you."

Instead of really truly hearing, I shout back out of frustration,

"I thought the purpose of writing the book was for everyone else to know that You love them. Isn't that at least part of the purpose of me writing the book?"

I am waiting for the doctor to come in and interrupt this conversation at any point.

God very quietly and calmly says;
"Daughter it's not your job to tell them. It's Mine."

Confessions of a control freak:
Learning that I need to live a life of balance and complete dependency on God has made me fully aware of my ongoing addiction to control. I become out of balance so easily. When my focus is placed anywhere other than the strong heartbeat and voice of my Creator.

The need to control! It's an addiction for me. I am thinking back to that moment I was in the hotel room at 'She Speaks' in the summer of 2010 wishing I had a story. A story that would be worth telling to others to prove that God works miracles. I knew that night that I was not a victim in my own story, rather that I had played a part.

I can now look back over the years and see how my need to control is linked to every part of my life. The lie and sin that kept me in such bondage was my desperate need to control. I thought I was in control of God. My actions would determine whether He could or would love me. My actions would determine if He would forgive me. Legalism and following rules was something I could 'do'. I was in control. I thought I was in control of relationships. I got married the first time to prove to others that I could do it. Even if common sense and circumstances said I wouldn't. When it didn't work out, I said I would never do it again. I was in control. I determined that I had messed up and didn't deserve to be happy in a marriage. I didn't get to be blessed by God because I had messed up. God hated divorce and therefore God hated me. This struggle in marriage would go on for years and years for me. Knowing God was blessing me each and every day with an amazing husband, but knowing I didn't deserve it. I wanted to be in control and call the shots so as not to be caught off guard or get hurt. I would rather forgo becoming a mom - it was one area I knew I wouldn't be able to control completely.

However, God knew what I needed and what was best for me. He wanted me to see that there was forgiveness, love, grace, and second chances. For I would give all this and more to two little boys and someday I would make the connection that it was available for me too. I wanted to be in control of my career, to be able to work when I wanted to, where I wanted. Where did God want me? Home supporting my husband and two boys. So as to teach me that there is always a greater purpose, because His ways are not my ways. For the impact a family can have in this world for Jesus comes through having a healthy home. This was not something I would know unless I was willing to live it out. He needed me home as a wife and a mom. No matter how many times I would try and busy myself with something else to get 'out of' doing what He had asked me, it would ultimately come back to prove He needed me home.

I want to be in complete control of my body. I want to be in control of how it feels, what it does and to keep it from getting sick and breaking down. I want to control what others think of me. So I work as a people pleaser so that their thoughts, opinions and ideas of me and about me are good. That way I am in control of all circumstances in my life. Boy does this feel weird to type and get out. Overwhelming and freeing all at the same time! I believed in the falsehood that I could dictate what would be. That if I planned, worked hard enough then everything would be the way it needed to be. I look back on all the energy exerted to live this lifestyle and it grieves me. All that energy misdirected and misused. Yet I am humbled in this moment to know God knew. He knew it would play out this way.

This brings up emotions of embarrassment, shame and disappointment in me, but to allow these emotions to rule me is to allow pride to win. I am in desperate need of transforming from the 'need to be in control' to the original design of having self-control.

Giving up control:

Whoever finds their life will lose it, and whoever loses their life for my sake will find it. Matthew 10:39

Which is NOT something I can do. But. God can. I have to be willing to admit my weaknesses and lay them down; this is NOT easy for me. But God enables me.

I need self-control in my life. I am not strong enough on my own to resist going into the shoe store and filling a lonely feeling with a new pair of shoes. I am not strong enough on my own to not eat food to deal with the stresses of life. Without self-control I can't keep my mouth from saying things I shouldn't. I want a clear mind free of excessive thoughts, so I need self-control. A mind that is clear of prideful thoughts, fearful and anxious thoughts. A mind that is free from jealous, angry and doubting thoughts.

Like a city whose walls are broken down is a man
who lacks self-control. Proverbs 25:28

A broken life! A chaotic mess! At times I feel like a raging bull that is clumsy in word and deed that does first and thinks later. I feel like I am pulled around by my emotions and then have a lot of cleaning up to do.

Such wisdom in this Proverb;
But a wise man keeps himself under control. Proverbs 29:11

I want that. Self-control.

The shortest member of the T-Squad had a difficult morning with keeping his words and actions in check. He was lacking in the area of self-control. I so get him, because he's just like his momma! We were out in the back yard raking up leaves and my son declared, "Mommy I am going to be good." I responded, "Well then stop talking about being good and just do it!" As those words left my mouth they hit my heart hard. It was as if I was speaking those words to myself at the same time. I might be a big girl on the outside... but it is the heart today that so feels like a little girl who wants to just sit in the corner, or hey maybe even the closet and just cry. But no I have to choose to have self-control. Choose to have a right attitude. Choose to act and NOT react. Choose to be peaceful, loving, kind, gentle, and calm. Quit just talking about living purposefully and do it! "Well stop talking about being good and just do it!" I was encouraged as those words left my mouth, encouraged to join my son in living them out. In His strength I can!

I need to have discipline in my thoughts, my emotions, and willingness to allow God's will to become my will.

Discipline can be interpreted as a naughty word… but before I write it off as that, I need to go a little further.

Discipline should be a tool, not a master over our lives. Again there is balance and swinging too far to one side makes discipline too heavy.

The enemy has deceived many of us by allowing us to think we can never live in balance by celebrating and being disciplined all at the same time.

For God did not give us a spirit of timidity, but a spirit of power, of love and of **self-discipline**. *2 Timothy 1:7 (emphasis mine)*

God created us to seek balance and then live in it.

"If you will see yourself the way He sees you (finished) then you will become what He says you are. He calls us disciplined and self-controlled and we must have that godly image if we want a life of freedom."[1]

Do I believe discipline is freedom?

God continues to teach me about balance. I am to be seeking it in all areas of my life.

The purpose of discipline is to make us more like Jesus.

Jesus is an amazing role model of balance.

Balance is not about oppression or manipulation. Balance was created so we could truly experience the freedom of a grace and love filled relationship with our Creator.

Discipline should always be a selfish thing. Discipline is a one on one thing with God. It is NOT my job, role, or purpose to discipline anyone else. My convictions are not everyone else's.

Self-control should always focus on self!

God fuels the power for discipline and self-control.

*But the fruit of the Spirit is love, joy, peace, patience, kindness, goodness, faithfulness, gentleness, **self-control**; against such things there is no law. Now those who belong to Christ Jesus have crucified the flesh with its passions and desires. If we live by the Spirit, let us also walk by the Spirit. Galatians 5:22-25 (New American Standard Bible) (emphasis mine)*

Is it really about coming to the awareness of not being in control? To think that I thought I was in control seems foolish now. I am still very aware of the fear of not being in control prior to the realization that it is way more calm and peaceful to not be in control. To be stripped of that seems so overwhelming and yet so right at the same time. I am really at peace. I really 'like' where I am at now. For my identity is not found in what I do, or who I am but whose I am. I am found in Him. Running, striving, achieving, and doing does not lead me to finding myself in Him. For me it distracted me. It kept me from knowing and hearing Him.

When Love takes over, fear, worry, doubt, anxiety, the need to please, the striving for perfection, the addiction to be in control becomes less. That last one had been my biggest issue. Control. Wanting it, needing it, knowing I couldn't function without it. Control over my thoughts, control over my health, my actions, the words coming out of my mouth, my relationships, my boys, control over the church I attended. Is that not the craziest thing in the whole world? It's not even realistic. Seriously who in their right mind thinks they can be in control of everything? That's just it - it was all a mind/head knowledge thing for me. I wasn't allowing the One who lived in my heart to rule and reign. I wasn't living fully in love with the One who loved me. It is impossible to allow God to be in control of my life while I am battling Him every day for control over everything in my life. I am shocked and relieved all in one breath. I have been stripped of so much to come to this level of understanding.

Understanding I am not, but He is. I am not in control. But He is. I am not perfect, but He is! I am not strong and capable of all things, but He is. I can't hold it together emotionally, but my Creator does every second of everyday and won't stop.

The sun is shining outside; it beckons me to come. Come walk in it. Come enjoy the heat of the sun. May I know that there is freedom in Him. A freedom to live fully. A freedom that comes with grace and love to endure through all of life. A place of balance, joy, contentment. A place that was created for me to find and know. The two of us in relationship.

My Prayer: Lord my life long struggle with You has been me wanting to be in control of everything. I am coming to learn that this is not how You designed it to be. Me wanting to be in control and having self-control are NOT the same thing. I desire self-control. I know the testimony of You living in me will produce just that. Help me to let go and let You! Amen.

Transition to Run

One of the things I have learned on this journey is that I was worried about everyone else knowing that God loved them when I really didn't know it for myself. Who am I? Now if that isn't covered in some nasty looking pride I am not sure what is! Is that not being a total hypocrite? Isn't that one of the main problems with the church? So many people say they want nothing to do with the church because it is filled with hypocrites. Why in the world would I be so focused on speaking, writing and sharing a message that I didn't truly know in my heart and soul? Seriously?! I have no business telling you that Jesus loves you if I don't know that He loves me. If one doesn't know they are loved, doesn't truly have the 100 percent pure unconditional love from God, their Creator, they cannot love, because they are not able to love, this is His design. And I sure the heck can't live my life on purpose, if I don't know what the 'on purpose' part of that equation is.

So I go back to the question, **"Do you know I love you?"** I need to know this. Imagine what our world would look like if people all knew this for themselves. So here is where the really difficult part of this whole book thing comes in for me. I started out thinking I was writing a book to let you know that God loves you. I ended up writing about the journey I am living to know that my God loves me. I truly believe we each have that same journey to live. Yours will be filled with different stops, colors, smells and issues. However the underlying theme will be the same. Jesus loves you. Jesus loves me. Jesus loves us! I am thankful for the enduring love of my Creator that continues this journey. For pride can still tend to entangle me and entice me with a lie here or there. My eyes can end up on 'others' and their journey and think it's not right because it's not like mine. His pure unfailing love changes us into our original design. We become in His love that which He intended for us to be.

The song:
'Jesus Loves Me
Jesus loves me.
This I know.
For the Bible tells me so (the Word, speak to me, personal, intimate, for me)
Little ones to Him belong. (those that are humble, pride is too big and gets in the way)
They are weak but He is strong (my weakness is just what He wants/needs/desires, He created me weak, it does not surprise Him. His strength balances me)
Yes Jesus loves me
Yes Jesus loves me
Yes Jesus loves me
The Bible tells me so.'

When we know we are loved we can love one another.

And this is love: that we walk in obedience to his commands.
As you have heard from the beginning, his command is that
*you **walk in love**.2 John 6 (emphasis mine)*

How can I walk in love? What does walking in love look like?
I re-read 2 John and this speaks to my heart;
His command is that you walk in love.

Walk in love?

Could it be putting the needs of others before yours?

Maybe it's paying for the Starbucks' order behind you.

Could it be choosing to point out the positive things your children are doing instead of the negative?

Maybe it's holding the door open for the person walking into the store.

Could it be doing something without anyone knowing?

Maybe it's staying silent when your flesh wants to speak.

Could it be speaking words of encouragement to your spouse?

Maybe it's forgiving someone who has hurt you deeply.

Could it be befriending someone new?

Maybe it's smiling more today.

It is 10:30am I am sitting in a hotel room in California. I am with The Engineer tagging along on a business trip. I just got back from doing some 'therapy' in the workout room. While running on the treadmill this morning the song '*Made to Love*'[1] by TobyMac came on with the lyrics; '*Anything I would give up for you, Everything, I'd give it all away.*' As I listened I desired those to be more than just words. Make them the truth. I don't want to say I have faith and not live it out. I don't want to say I am submissive and willing to give God all of me and not live it out.

And when I have trained. When I am ready. Then I will run.

"If you have learned to sit, stand, and walk in God, it is time to start running in and with God."[2]

It's raining outside. The world is so full of color. As I drove home this morning from delivering the boys to school I realized I get to write today. I remember when the dread of that, the anxiety of that, the worry of that consumed me. I GET to write today. I get to seek God in this venue. A place, a time, it's just God and me. Not me striving to get in a certain amount of minutes or words. Or me trying to get it just right and perform for Him. Not me stressing about how the chapters are coming along or if I am forming proper sentences. It's me finding Him.

My heart hurts in remembrance of my false belief system of me creating God to be judgmental, harsh, His arms crossed, looking down upon me. Shaking His head in disgust wishing I would get my act together and stop screwing up. It pains me to think I created this, how I allowed this false belief to consume me, to keep me prisoner. I was stuck in the need to seek perfection, to be in control, I was lost in pride. But love endures and never stops pursuing me, and never will. Love seeks.

It's been awhile… a long while since I sat down to 'purposefully' write. The reason; the summer was filled with lots of fun times. I could have made time… but I didn't. I could dwell on that… but I won't. That's grace… that is moving on. And living in this moment. I can't go back and change it. So I will be here. I will write this morning.

I can feel part of myself just wishing this book was done already. Really what is taking so long? It's a 'me' thing. But really how do I just buckle down and get it done? I can sense myself wanting it done so I can move onto something else, and I feel guilty for that. Something else that would be respected, noticed, and, appreciated by others. Yikes! That is far too much confession. Seriously. There it is in words. Writing is not contributing to our family, if anything it takes time away. Even after dabbling these couple of years I still feel like I am in way over my head.

"Nichole relax! Take a deep breath. Don't worry, or stress it is all there. You have lived out the pages of this book. I will bring it together, trust me Nichole. I love you and I am with you. I will bring organization to what feels chaotic. I will bring structure."

God has been SO patient with me. And He knew I would fight Him on this book thing! I am still in awe.

It's so quiet here this morning. I can hear the tumble and squeak of the dryer as the towels toss around. The boys are at school. It seems like a pretty messy idea to me to write a book when you never have and the thought of the finished pages seems overwhelming impossible… at least this morning.

I love to read. I love to read all kinds of books. Books encourage, they challenge, they help us question. Books take our mind and hearts to places we might not choose to go on our own. Books are filled with words. My words are really not my own. The words in this book share my life, thus far. And maybe that's why I am struggling with the idea of this book never really being finished. My life will keep on. So the end of the book will be a page that catches the reader up to the point at which I end it. Better yet the point at which God ends it. There is hesitation in my mind and heart to that idea. For as much as I have not enjoyed parts of this book writing process, I am aware of the closeness to my Creator in which it has brought me. I don't wish to leave, or walk away, or better yet to run out ahead. I desire to stay close. But I question myself. My ability to stay without a tether. A tether that yields obedience.

My Prayer: I pray Lord that this morning I will not walk out of Your presence, but hold tight to Your hand, knowing that to do life I have to be in step with You. I need You. Your strength for today. To live for the very purpose of being in relationship with You. To seek You and not myself. To seek Your heart with such passion and addiction that while doing so others see You and come running too. I love You Lord. May this journey from the comfort to the unknown continue. May I be teachable. May I follow Your lead. May my hand hold tight to Yours. Knowing and trusting that You will lead in Your perfect way and time. Amen.

PART 4:

Run

Because You Love Me

Did you know that 'avocado hand injury' is a real thing? Google it. I can now join the 'special club'. Last Wednesday night I was trying to remove a pit out of the avocado. The paring knife, (that The Engineer keeps nice and sharp for me) went deep into my hand severing an artery, ulnar nerve, muscle, and tendons. When I met with the doctor on Thursday, he said I could do nothing and eventually lose the full use of my hand or I could let him repair it. Hard decision there! So Friday morning he operated and repaired my hand. I cannot use my right hand at all. I will be visiting a hand clinic for therapy. This morning I am questioning how am I to write?

God's message to me:

"The point of this journey/book/relationship Nichole is for you to know I love you. God- your Creator-your Savior-your Healer- your Rescuer- your Redeemer- the One- loves you Nichole. You have to know that."

"Even though you were writing the book it was never really about the book."

My response:

"And here I thought I was writing this book for others."

Writing the book and this whole process was for me to know I am loved. This morning on my run I am realizing I struggle with keeping some of

God's love for myself… like that would selfish or something. Hence being okay with writing the book if it was for someone else.

"Be careful My daughter, you have a tendency to think that My Words are for everyone else. Not always in a prideful way, but rather that you don't deserve to hear them. That you don't deserve to be quiet and soak in My love. Please know in your head and heart that you are Mine and I love and adore you. The message of the book is for you."

(After the avocado incident.) To type again! It's been awhile since my fingers clicked these lettered tabs on my laptop. I come to write. I sit correctly in front of the keyboard, positioned in front of the 'J' as I was taught in keyboarding class in high school. I remember this morning back to the days when I wanted to just type out this book, finish it, be done so that I could move on to the 'next thing'. The next exciting and glamorous thing. The thing that held more excitement, more people, more attention. Today I am here realizing the foolishness of my own self. For this was never about a book. It had nothing to do with chapters, words, pages, or sentence structure. It was all about the Creator coming close. Close to the heart of a girl who desperately needed Him. The heart that would need to be reminded again and again that it is safe. Trusting would come. Faith would develop.

Last night Team Hamblin watched *Despicable Me.*[1] I distinctly remember when that movie came out how against it I was. It was all in the title. Why in the world would someone want to watch a movie with the word 'despicable' in the title? Especially a movie for kids and family. Last night we were getting all cozy for the movie and Tanner asked, "What does despicable mean?" So I told him that it means, "Gross, bad, icky, not good, not liked because it's really bad." Tanner responded with, "Then why are we watching this movie? It sounds like it's not a good movie for us to watch." I told him that a few of my mommy friends said that it was actually a really good movie. I tell him we should see if it's about someone who changes. So we watched it and sure enough it is one of my favorite movies! Love. Love changes people's lives. Gru, the main 'villain bad dude' is changed because of love. At the end Gru reads the girls the story he wrote, in that he shares that they changed his heart. Love changes people's hearts!

God has the ability to see past the outside appearance of things. Past the cover of a book. Past the title of a movie. Past the actions of people. To the core of what is. He sees the heart of His creation. And loves. This love transforms His creation back into their original design.

One of my favorite passages in the Bible has to be Isaiah chapter 43. There is so much Love and greatness packed into it.

*Since you are precious and honored in my sight, and **because** **I love you**. Isaiah 43:4a (emphasis mine)*

He says I am precious. I am honored in His sight. This takes away that old vision I had standing before Him. And He says it's all because He loves me.

My most favorite words in the whole Bible are those four words. ***Because I love you.***

*"Fear not, for **I have redeemed you;** **I have summoned you by name; you are mine.** When you pass through the waters, **I will be with you;** and when you pass through the rivers, **they will not sweep over you.** When you walk through the fire, **you will not be burned;** the flames will not set you ablaze. **Do not be afraid, for I am with you** Isaiah 43:1-2, 5 (emphasis mine)*

Because of His love for me, God has called my name. I am His. He has redeemed me. God is with me. He promises to protect me.

Everyone who is called by my name,
whom I created for my glory,
whom I formed and made. *Isaiah 43:7 (emphasis mine)*

Because God loves me He made and created me for His glory.

I, even I, am the Lord,
*and apart from me there is no **savior**.*
I have revealed and saved and proclaimed—
I am the Lord, your Holy One,
Israel's Creator, your King." Isaiah 43:11-12, 16 (emphasis mine)

Because God loves me, He saved me. He is my Savior.

The people I formed for myself *that they may*
proclaim my praise. Isaiah 43:21 (emphasis mine)

Because God loves me, He formed me for Himself.

God didn't just create me and place me here on this earth for no purpose.

When He went to the cross for me it wasn't just so I could be saved and then sit on a pew in some stuffy church and stand and sing songs, and sit and listen to a sermon. Nope it wasn't! And sometimes my little girlie mind wonders if that even crossed our Jesus' mind when He walked that hill to then be nailed to the cross.

I think He was thinking of more.

I think He was thinking of how much He adored His people. How much He loved us. How much He needed us to know that love.

For Him it didn't stop at the moment of salvation. He wasn't just trying to win our souls.

He wasn't trying to get us to go to church.

He wasn't hoping for a 15 minute one time prayer session with us.

Nope.

Rather I believe He wanted more.

He wanted us to know that He adored us. He loved us!

Because of His great love for us. Ephesians 2:4a

Because He loves us He wants more for us.

More than we have experienced to this point.

More than we have allowed ourselves to see, feel, and do.

He has more for us.

I was asked ever so politely by my Jesus to sit in the spring of 2010 and it took until the middle of summer 2010 for me to truly hear it. My Jesus can get loud if He needs to be. There was no mistake it was His voice. Now I would be lying if I told you I took those months to truly try to 'discern' if it was His voice asking me to sit or not, but friends I was so not discerning anything, I was in my usual pattern of running. I was thinking to my sweet stubborn self, '*if I keep moving and doing this good Jesus girl stuff, He can't possibly stop me!*' Seriously to look back on that I laugh, I laugh!

Fast-forward through a whole lotta days, hours, and months and yes even years and what do I have to say...

I am so in love with Jesus.

Because He loves me.

When you sit on a bench and all is taken away, the world is quiet, and life becomes not about you - you realize His love. You feel His love. You know for the first time you were created for His love. And this love is what fuels you to be.

I had this whole love thing backwards for years. I thought the most important thing was that I loved Jesus.

Nope.

Rather the importance is that He loves me.

I have had a lot of time with Him, and for that I am not the same girl He placed on the bench a couple of years ago. You can almost hear friends and family shouting, "Praise God!"

'I'm everything I am
Because you loved me'[2]

Why can't I seem to finish this book? Will I ever? Isn't it supposed to be finished? Finished now there is a super hard word to type out right now. I am sitting here at the bar in our kitchen. I can hear her paws clicking the tile floor she is deciding whether she will eat. I have just got off the phone with the vet. Our brown girl dog is too sick. She can't keep living like this. Tomorrow. Lord this hurts. The hard parts in life are supposed to hurt. Aware of my emotions. Writing a book is hard and death is hard. Really? How can I even list those both in the same sentence? Those are two totally different things. Hard must have a scale, but my hard won't be another's. For what I find difficult might not even evoke emotion in you, and yet we are called to stand next to each other. As I listened to others share their story their hard has been way harder than my hard. Or is hard just different? And not to be understood. But to trust. Deep calming breaths I take. I really don't want to do this hard. To have to let go. She has been in our lives for 12 plus years. Prayers of preparation are lifted, for the next moments. To live fully in these moments.

Choosing to know because He loves me I can go through hard moments.

My Prayer: I had things out of order for many years. Thank You Lord for Your enduring Love and patience with me. I falsely believed that my love for You was the focus. During the quiet time on the bench I have come to learn that the order is; be loved and then love. Love has changed me. Love has taught me I can do hard things. Because You Love me! Amen.

Marathon/Endurance/Pacer

Iam in California. I am typing on my laptop that is on my table working on this book at our rental home in southern California. I told The Engineer I would follow him anywhere he wanted to go, 'as long as it's not California'. I was born and bred in the Pacific Northwest (PNW) and it's what makes me the most comfortable. The rivers, the mountains, the wildlife and for some odd reason I manufactured a very unlikable image of the state of California. Cause it's easier to cast judgment than it is to find out the truth. I have always pictured California as the land of flash cars, mansions, and suntanned perfectly chiseled bodies. "Cali", where more focus was spent on the outward appearance and nothing was ever real or genuine. I am good or actually really bad at creating images of things, ones in which the Creator is always intent on proving me wrong. Or to say it nicer, reveal the truth to me. So He has brought me here to California to continue to work on my book. Somewhere I never wanted to be, writing a book I never sought out to write. HA! The irony; God is funny! I have lessons to learn here. I have areas to grow in. I have a relationship with Jesus in which I want to go deeper. God would not ask me to come somewhere that He was not. Love doesn't do that.

Life takes you places. We are living in a tiny little town up at 4000 feet. The very first time I went out and ran here my lungs were burning so bad. As I am run I wonder if this is where the book will wrap itself together.

I was sucked in via the adorable faces of kids on a screen. World Vision visited our church today and they are putting together a team that will raise money and run the L.A. Marathon for water for kids in countries where clean water is not available. Against my own thoughts, the concerns of The Engineer and all sanity, I signed up. This will be my very first marathon. I am convinced that I am stubborn enough to do it. I will run 26.2 miles on Sunday March 15, 2015. I have NEV-ER run this distance before. It is overwhelming, intimidating, scary, and nerve wracking. But I can't handle knowing that there are people in our world who don't have water. I can't stand not doing anything about it. So I will run.

I began training for the LA Marathon. I very quickly realize that this amount of running, and these distances is not something I can do. Not in my strength. I was out running one morning and in desperate need of some encouragement.

But only God. 1 Corinthians 3:7

Those three words. His power. My need for dependence.

"Whether you believe you can or believe you can't, you're probably right."[1]

Marathon training takes commitment. It takes discipline to go out and run allotted miles for that day and get your total in for the week. I found myself out there for hours logging miles - in all kinds of weather.

No discipline seems pleasant at the time, but painful… Later
on, however, it produces a harvest of righteousness and peace
for those who have trained by it. Hebrews 12:11

Discipline has never been pleasant for me. Not being able to run when I wanted to, and having to wait, rest and heal was hard. But because of those times I know I can do hard things. Like train for a marathon. Goals take discipline.

"The people I love, I call to account—prod and correct and guide
so that they'll live at their best. Up on your feet, then! About
face! Run after God!" Revelation 3:19 (The Message)

On my run this morning I was thinking about how in the past I kept busy 'running' from shame, imperfections, and failures. What was I running to? People, food, shopping. This was not the Creator's design. I am learning that I was born to run. Run with God, for God, and most importantly into God's arms. I truly want God's will for me, because then I am right where I am supposed to be. Surrounded by Him.

Running these long distances for me wasn't about speed. I wasn't focused on how fast I could knock out the miles, but my main goal was to finish the miles. I needed endurance. Over a period of time I built up endurance. It took patience.

He has made everything beautiful in its time. Ecclesiastes 3:11a

God's love for me is an enduring love. God knew the outcome, but He also knew every moment in between. Today I'm aware that Love has stayed knowing, knowing all about me and that makes me more aware of the depth of Love. More aware of the purity of Love.

The LORD will fulfill His purpose for me; Your love, O LORD, endures
forever - do not abandon the works of Your hands. Psalm 138:8

God will do it, because He said He would and He keeps His promises! Amen

For it is God who works in you to will and to act according
to His good purpose. Philippians 2:13

God uses everyday moments to improve my character. He works to free me from bitterness, doubt, fear, worry, anger, jealously, selfishness, pride, perfectionism, comparison, people pleasing, and rule following. God works to free me from myself. He knew just what I needed - patience, time, commitment, and most importantly His enduring Love! He knew all about me and also my failures. Love will not give up on me.

For the LORD is good and His love endures forever. Psalm 100:5a

Love endures hard things like a cross on a hill. Every word, insult, rolling of the eyes, hateful heart, spit, crown of thorns, mocking, beating, the cross, and separation from the Father. Love endured. Through His example I see that enduring is possible. With His help I can do hard things. My current hard thing is to be a momma who has enduring love for a little guy who, while aiming for the toilet hoses down the shower curtain on accident. I can do hard things!

I'm reading in Psalm 136 this morning *His love endures forever*. What does endure really mean?

en dure [2] *verb (used with object)*
- to hold out against; sustain without impairment or yielding; undergo
- to bear without resistance or with patience; tolerate
- to admit of; allow; bear

en dure *verb (used without object)*
- to continue to exist; last
- to support adverse force or influence of any kind; suffer without yielding; suffer patiently
- to have or gain continued or lasting acknowledgment or recognition, as of worth, merit or greatness

As I am training a super amazing friend joins me on my runs. Having someone to talk with on the runs make them go by much faster. The runs with my friend keep me from 'hearing' all the crazy thoughts bouncing around in my head. I want to finish the marathon training and race injury free so we usually stick to a two minute run with a 30 second walk. This helps build my endurance and keep a pretty good pace. Keeping a steady pace helps your body to not burn out. I suffer from the 'speed really fast and get ahead right at the start' syndrome. I desperately need a pacer. So I use an app on my phone that reminds me of my pace.

Keep in step with the Spirit. Galatians 5:25

Looking back I can see all the times I ran out too far ahead of God. I thought I could do it on my own, that I didn't need a pacer. During those times I would quickly become tired and not be able to maintain the pace.

Do you not know?
Have you not heard?
The Lord is the everlasting God,
the Creator of the ends of the earth.
He will not grow tired or weary,
and his understanding no one can fathom.
He gives strength to the weary
and increases the power of the weak.
Even youths grow tired and weary,
and young men stumble and fall;
but those who hope in the Lord
will renew their strength.
They will soar on wings like eagles;
they will run and not grow weary,
they will walk and not be faint. Isaiah 40: 28-31

It really is in my best interest to stay with Jesus, my pacer.

Pacing yourself works to guard your energy, allowing you to finish the race. A lot can happen in 26.2 miles. Especially in your thoughts! I told myself I was crazy, that I wasn't prepared for this, that I couldn't do it, what was I thinking? I wasn't a runner. I made all sorts of internal bold claims. I wanted to quit. My body wanted to quit. During a little 'come to Jesus' moment in the porta potty God made it pretty clear that I was to get back out there and finish. Thanks to a very committed Runner Girl who endured the race next to me the entire time, I made it across the finish line. There waiting for me were two other faithful Runner Girls cheering me on. I finished my first marathon. Tired, sweaty and sore, I finished. It was hard. But I did it. I can do hard things. With God!

*I run in the path of your commands, for you have
broadened my understanding. Psalm 119:32*

My eyes have to be fixed on Him. On Him for 'the course' of my race.

For Christ's love compels us. 2 Corinthians 5:14a

My Prayer: I know that You have a specific 'course' for me. I am to stay focused and intent on that one. Run, stay in step with You as my pacer, and keep moving. With the intent to finish strong, the attitude of knowing there is a purpose and reason to run. For I know I have tested the endurance of Your love and You have not lost patience with me. That is something I can't truly understand. There needs to exist a healthy awe and reverence and here I am this morning in that place. Taking in Your presence here with me, a sinner who struggles with pride, judgment, control, and perfection.

You are here with me. You Lord are the author and perfecter of my faith. Thank You for continually reminding me who You are and who I am in You. You are perfect and amazing Love! Enduring Love, You haven't grown weary of pursuing me. May I be in step with You in this relationship. Thank You for setting a perfect pace, and for guiding the steps. Amen.

Lost in Love

There are things we think we can control in this world.

Schedules, appointments, to do lists, children, people, the church.

We think we can organize, structure and shape how things are.

Should we pause?

When we focus on the controlling of such things we might be missing something.

Because maybe love really doesn't work that way.

Maybe love is different.

Maybe it doesn't just show up when we think it should.

Maybe it doesn't happen within certain walls or certain buildings.

It's not something we can control.

We are not in charge of love and yet we think we are.

I am guilty.

Guilty of thinking I loved enough. Loved appropriately. Loved the right way.

And yet love doesn't have rules.

But we give it rules.

I limited love to my way of thinking.

We say it should feel a certain way. It should behave this way. It should meet these requirements. We shape love. We mould love to our standards, our comfort level.

For love is who it is.

I am a learner. A learner of love.

Love that shows up unannounced.

Love that doesn't have an agenda.

Love that truly brings a different perspective.

Love that isn't of me.

Love that truly is pure. Not hindered. Not contained. Not limited.

Love.

Love. We humans have messed up that word. Love is more than a word. Love is perfect, holy, pure, righteous, true, unconditional, completing, full, whole love. We were created for love. When we experience love we feel content and peaceful. We know what joy is. We know why we were created. To be in love with our Creator. Those seven words just hit me! To be IN LOVE with You. Relationship. We are in the relationship with love itself. Love. We join in. We are in. We remain in. Being 'in love' is being in Him. Right where we were created to be! This is the part of writing that I enjoy the most, knowing Him more. Hearing from Him. God showing me my original design. To be in love with Him! When we are 'in love' with Him everything else in our lives will be in balance. Our health, our relationships, our purpose. The radio is playing in the back ground. I hear the words, *'She will be loved.'* I will be loved by God, because that is what He created me for. He created me to love.

Help my mind and heart to get totally lost in Your love.

Learning to trust someone takes time. Trust happens inside the intimacy of a relationship. Dependent on our past for some of us trust takes even more time. There might be times or happenings that led to people hurting our trust. Causing us to question if we could ever trust again.

There are questions with no answers this side of heaven.

There are problems too big and overwhelming to shoulder alone.

There is pain underneath an old scar.

There are tears that need to be shed.

There are doubts, worries, fears, and 'ickies' that are not as bad in the daylight, but night time seems so long.

You want to fix it, but don't know how.

Running would be easier.

Screaming seems like an okay response.

The lump in your throat won't go away.

You just have to trust Him, hold on tighter and wait in His love.

"Daughter I have this. I love you and I know what's best. Trust me Nichole. Know that you are mine and that I protect and provide for You."

Lost in love.

I am totally into Him.

It won't always appear on the outside, because I still get in the way.

And my shoe loving girlie self makes mistakes.

But I do know, I love the way He loves me.

He loves in His way and in His time.

It takes my breath away.

To experience His love is to see that the sky is blue, bluer than blue.

I tend to get in the way of myself.

But even then, love wins.

Strength doesn't just appear; it has to be applied.

Fear isn't going to go away, it has to be conquered.

Words might not come when you need them, so silence will speak.

Every tear and prayer is worth it.

Never giving up hope.

Allowing Him to work it out in His time.

I won't ever have it right, or perfect.

But the one thing I do know.

I want to be lost.

Lost in love.

Things that get in the way can be annoying and frustrating.

Finding out that you are in your own way... now that is hard to swallow.

I am in the way.

I asked and even cried out on the top of the country road while running this morning for Him to just pick me up and move me out of my own way.

But He responded, He will not.

He wants me to learn to move out of my own way.

He says its grace.

I say it seems too hard.

He says I will truly know He loves me.

I ask again are You sure?

I don't want to be in my own way.

But I am.

I need to move.

I will move.

But it's hard.

It's hard admitting you're in your own way.

Accepting love and grace isn't always easy.

"Nichole live one moment at a time. Take each breath. Rest in Me. Know that I am in control. I will guide and direct each moment. You don't have to have everything planned out. Trust me. I am in control."
Trust Your love for me.

Therefore love is the fulfillment of the law. Romans 13:10

Is this love thing all there really is to it? Being loved and loving. What we are here for. To discover the One who created us, knows us and loves us. In the moments that we are aware of this truth we are truly alive. Truly breathing.

I'm not saying that I have this all together, that I have it made. But I am well on my way, reaching out for Christ, who has so wondrously reached out for me. Friends, don't get me wrong: By no means do I count myself an expert in all of this, but I've got my eye on the goal, where God is beckoning us onward—to Jesus. I'm off and running, and I'm not turning back. Philippians 3:12-14 (The Message)

I am sitting here thinking of the beginning of this book journey and how much I fought the whole process, not truly seeing it for what it really was. To now know it had nothing to really do with a book, but rather a love relationship. I am amazed at how much God loves me. How He would take the time to truly secure that in my heart. I won't waste His time trying to question why I fought Him so much in the beginning or why He didn't give up on me, because I am learning that's how love works. Outside our human understanding. There are not boundaries or rules to love.

Here in Tehachapi there is a glider airport. You get in the glider and an airplane will pull you up into the air and then you release from each other and you ride the thermals. There is something so natural, pure and genuine about watching a glider fly. It's what it looks like when you watch one of God's children live free in grace and love. They enjoy the ride, they trust where they are. To know you are completely where you are to be. Peace. Peace in the deepest part of your soul. Nothing can get us there but love. Love has a strength and courage that pushes past and through what we might consider not possible. But again all things are possible through Him, and so again God trumps. There are no excuses when love enters the picture. Nothing can inhibit that which love motivates. Love conquers. Love wins. All the time! Every time. And so why do we choose anything else? We want control. We want to prove our worth. We want to make sure we are acceptable. Love is patient while we figure it out. Love doesn't have a prerequisite. Love wants, it rather needs us empty. Love works best when we have nothing. The amazing thing is that love knows our humanness and that we will struggle with this. True heart felt peace and joy comes and overtakes us when we realize that we don't have to struggle or fight for love. We need to accept. But that seems so passive. How can that be? Why in the world would a Creator, God, create something just for His pleasure? May we be reminded that's love. It's not within our human comprehension to understand. We are meant to just accept.

After years of asking, '*Why me?*' I finally sat down and looked at the screen, put my fingers to the keys and let my fingers move from my heart, not my head.

My Prayer: You love me with Your enduring love that sees me through Your most holy Son Jesus. May I know today this love, the love that has conquered all of sins, traps and even death itself, so that I can live free. May I know my freedom is found in remaining in You and Your great love for me. May I know today this wonderful love. Your love that has surrounded me, breathed life into me, and knows me so well. May I live out of this love that You have for me. May I truly be aware of it today. Your love. May my eyes see it. May my ears hear it. May my heart experience it. Thank You for continuing to bring me closer and teaching me that I was created for You. Thank You for the safety of this place. I love You Lord, Amen.

Run-Rest-Repeat

Hard. Life is often like that. Moments, days, weeks, seasons or even years where we just can't make it without Him. This is purposeful design. I was created with a desperate need to rely on His love for me. Without it I can't do anything. This would be an ongoing lesson for me to learn.

There are times that I would be healthy enough to run. Then there would be times I was supposed to be resting and letting my body heal. Times that were determined by God. He usually had to be pretty direct with me as I was often intent on just pushing through the pain.

I was running my second half marathon for the month along the Columbia River in the Pacific Northwest. One of the most gorgeous runs ever! I was about seven miles in when I lost feeling from the waist down; both of my legs went numb. Thanks to an amazing God who knew I would find myself in this moment. He had positioned a Runner Girl on each side of me. One was a doctor the other a nurse. I couldn't have had better care. I wasn't sure what was going on. But with the help of my friends, crying out in fear, tears running down my face and my mind just reminding my legs to keep moving, I finished. This would be the last time I ran.

The leg numbness was joined by other symptoms. I spent months visiting doctors, trying medications, having MRI's, trying physical therapy, and more. One night the pain in my lower back became very intense. The Engineer took me to the hospital where the ER doctor informed me I had cauda equina syndrome and admitted for emergency back surgery.

I woke the morning after surgery with a visit from the Neurosurgeon. She informed me she was elated that the surgery went as good as it did. When she first saw me in pre-op she was sure I was going to be paralyzed and leaving the hospital in a wheelchair.

But God had another plan.

And I thought the past few months before the surgery were hard. Not being able to run.

What we see on the outside is often strength and courage. While fear, pain, worry, doubts and a whole slew of other emotions are battling themselves out on the inside.

I will not sugar coat this.

I wanted something different.

I was mad, disappointed, frustrated, hurting and saddened.

I wanted to be the momma I always hoped to be for my boys.

I wanted to shoot hoops, play catch, run and kick the soccer ball.

I wanted to do all that and more.

Right now I can't dress myself. I have to ask for help with everything.

My biggest, largest, most deep fear is that my boys will grow up 'hating' their childhood because they were bogged down with a momma who 'couldn't'.

This isn't about whether my situation is 'worse or better' than someone else's. And it's not about what is and what isn't. It's about right now how I feel.

"Tyler and Tanner I love you like nothing else in this world. I love every detail and characteristic about you. I am sorry that life is really stinking hard right now. Because mommas are supposed to protect their little ones from the 'yuck' and un-fun of this world and I can't. I am sorry. I am so proud of your strength, courage and love".

This season would be one of the most humbling I had ever gone through. I would have even more of my pride stripped away. I would come to heads again with my desire to want to be in control. I would be reminded my desperate need for my Creator.

I go in for regular visits to my Neurosurgeon. I am doing all my physical therapy at home, as I can't drive. I am using one of those walker things to do laps around the house. I have to retrain the right leg, remind the nerve and muscles what they need to be doing. The Neurosurgeon is feeling positive with the direction, the continued healing and recovery is going. There are more positive days than negative. She said I could take a driving 'test' in two weeks and at the discretion of The Engineer (he's really liking the power she gave him). I can be cleared to drive on my good days. She stated today that she feels the next three to six months will give us the picture of where my leg will be as far as lifetime function.

I'd rather be running but instead 15-minute walker walks around my house continue.

Not being okay.

I have struggled coming to terms with what is going on with me.

It's a grieving of sorts. When the adrenaline of getting through something in survival mode and the 'rush' you come off of is now staring you in the face.

A new normal.

But not wanting to accept it!

God and I have been having some discussions. Admittedly I am doing a lot of question asking, stating how unfair it is and maybe even declaring how I feel shafted.

Loneliness and brokenness are being felt.

I am 'broken' physically waiting for that day when everything feels okay and right again.

However, in quiet moments knowing that the possibility of this being where I am at is most likely the new normal.

And having to be okay with not being okay.

I am trying to 'pay attention' to this life lesson for the mind, body and spirit.

I am fully aware I am standing in the center of a very peaceful location. But there are still questions and tears.

Struggling with trying to be okay when you really aren't okay is all right.

Even though I am unable to practice yoga right now I remember one of my yoga instructors sharing a passage about greed. Greed; defined as wanting to be in two places at once. For I have found myself not truly living in the moment and experiencing the gift of the moment I am in. I don't want to be here. I want to be where I was or far past this season.

It's been about three months since surgery and I put on my Runner Girl shirt and Tyler and I head outside for a WALK. For those of you who have dogs, especially dogs that love to go for walks, you know when you announce it and their back end starts a wagging and they are jumping and can't hold still to get their leash attached?! That was me. I was so elated to get outside of the house and into the fresh air. Tyler and I walked 2.38miles. I'm a long way from where I was in October, but hey I am moving in the right direction! Celebrate every breath, every step, every day.

It's been 277 days since I ran. The Runner's Magazine was in the mailbox today. This magazine still comes each month. It's a reminder of where I used to be. A current reality check of where I am. I know to be thankful that I am currently walking unassisted.

Jesus is reminding me today that He has an abundant life, a great amazing purpose filled life for me. I need to embrace that I am to be resting and healing right now. Allowing Him and others to fill in the gaps. That in the swollen body, (I am retaining more water than anyone else in the history of the world and could easily solve the drought in California), messy hair, not moving very fast, I can and will experience the grace and love of my Jesus. Not once I am healed and all better, but right now! I can experience Him right now.

DO YOU KNOW I LOVE YOU?

Let them renew their strength. Isaiah 41:1

I have watched *Yoga Is: A Transformational Journey.*[1] God has used yoga to help me learn about love. God uses what I would never have tried myself to meet me in the depths of my soul. Yoga has taught me to be aware of my thoughts, my body, and my very breath. I have learned to listen to my breath, to be still, to quiet my mind and thoughts, to breathe. Breathe through tension. To know times of rest are okay. Not right or wrong.

Last night as I stood assisted by my walker in a kitchen that didn't meet my standards of cleanliness, I realized I am comfortable in me, at peace in me, I know who I am, I am not right or wrong. I am His daughter and He loves me just the way I am. I have learned to know His love and become more at peace in Him and balanced in His joy and be content.

Not all doing is bad and wrong. For there are things in life we must do, but when our doing becomes more important than our being, we become out of balance, we become unhealthy in many ways. One of the things I enjoy about yoga is the teaching and instruction to be 100 percent present while practicing. To be aware of where you are, what you are doing, how your body feels, tuned into your breathing, to not let your thoughts run crazy. I am learning to carry this over into the other areas of my life. To be intent on 'being' where I am and doing what I am doing. Like writing right now. There are many thoughts competing for space in my head, and I am trying to focus on what I am hearing in my mind and heart that pertains to the book. We have all had minds filled with thoughts that would resemble a war scene. Bouncing, exploding, noise, smoke, chaos. To calm them is to focus more on being, than doing. To be aware of where you are, to breathe, to inhale with the intent of bringing in oxygen to power your body, to exhale to remove the toxins and carbon dioxide that your body does not need. What an amazing organ our lungs are. So many of us, myself included, have taken them for granted for years. Now I am not going to get all weird on you - but take a moment and think about it. I breathed for many years without ever paying attention to my breath. I took it for granted, because I was too busy 'doing' to notice. Which made me question how many other things did I miss because of being busy doing? Sounds, sights, and smells, how things feel to the touch. May I not go back. May I submit to the teaching of the Creator to live in balance. May I allow myself to 'be'. Be loved.

He is loving me to the point of surrender yet again.

Surrender to allow more 'healing'. Healing takes being still, rest, and time spent with God. God divinely orchestrates the process of healing. Healing properly is necessary to go on and be able to live out our purpose.

My personality tends to push through the pain instead of listening to my body. I will always be learning to rest and heal. Learning that the pain from healing and healing properly is what restores me to my original design. Being happy when everything is easy and comfortable is relying on myself. Choosing joy in the midst of the hard and unknown times is acknowledging the Strength that resides within me.

In You I rest, In You I found my hope.
In You I trust, You never let me go.
I place my life within Your hands alone.
Be still, my soul.[2]

In the moments that my thoughts run and outpace my heart I become fearful that all is not met. All is not okay. Thoughts that play what if, *'What if I won't ever be able to run again?'* Is this a reminder to be still? Are they my consequences of a life not obedient? So on this morning, despite those thoughts, concerns and questions that flee around in my mind, I am choosing to know He is in control. I am in His best interest. He cares for me. God adores and loves me. Those are not just thoughts, or words typed out, or even a mantra to repeat in times that are hard. Those are Truth. Those are Word. Living and active. For they pursue me and find me and meet me here. The question of will I be okay is one of fear and want. I desperately want to be okay. Can I try and tweak my want to make it a need? I need to be okay. I have a family; I have a book I'm writing. As I hear those words bounce right back to me they are rooted in fear, pride, and the need to control. Total submission is not completely clear to me in this, but I sense it will not include the question, "Will I be okay?" Because being aware of His Presence and living in relationship with Him is what I am here for, and that is 'okay.' That is purpose. Not a purpose I created for myself but His purpose for creating me. His perfect designed purpose for me. I am not sure that all that is within me will make it into words that fill pages of a book. And being okay, being content with that will be amazing. For again it will be the realization that the process was the purpose.

Run-Rest-Repeat.

I thank Him for teaching me perspective. Learning I am loved by God was not a destination to arrive at, rather a moment by moment place to abide in. Which slows the pace of things. For I am not running on ahead, rather holding tight to this moment wanting, needing to soak in all it has. Get every last drop out of it. It slows the breathing, opens the eyes, and steadies the pace of the heart. There is rhythm here. For a girl who feared the boredom and depth of quiet, I have found something much different. A place in which my thoughts are becoming more controlled. My eyes become more focused on Him and what He is doing.

My Prayer: I am thinking about all You have done for me. Rescued me. My deepest desire was to be rescued and loved, and yet for years I tried to hide the void. I didn't want to be weak. Having need in today's culture equals weakness. Dependence on a God who can't be seen? Trusting a love that can't be bought? How does that make sense? I spent so many minutes, hours, days, years striving to find joy, fulfillment, peace, contentment, and love. While You were right there waiting patiently for me. You knew. You knew every moment. You waited patiently. Thank You for helping me to learn there are times to run and times to rest. Amen.

Running on Purpose

When God asked me to sit it was to listen, learn and ultimately **know** I was loved by Him. Unconditional. Pure, righteous love! Once I know I am loved I need to love. Pass on Jesus to those around me. Love on them. To love and serve my family. Love them how they needed to be loved.

We love because He first loved us. 1 John 4:19

I desire to love like Jesus loves. I desire to be spreading Love!

Intense love does not measure, it just gives.[1]

I look forward to meeting Mother Teresa. I just wanna hug her. Tell her 'thank you' for living it out. I want to tell her I appreciate her amazing role model of living out the love of our Jesus. But until I get that opportunity I want to follow in the footsteps that she chose to follow in. I desire to be unselfish, to be giving, to be loving, to provide, and to care for.

I do feel very passionate about people. About loving them.

I don't want to talk about what's wrong with our schools, medical care, and government. I feel less like talking about how to fix them.

Keep on loving one another as brothers and sisters. Hebrews 13:1

I feel more called to live out what He's asking me to live out.

To love.

When I see a need, to meet it, or at least attempt to try.

When I see public schools that need a volunteer, to go and give the time.

When I see kids that are cold, to provide coats.

When I see a family struggling to put the basics in place, to get the basics to them.

When I see a woman hurting and lonely, I will listen.

When I see a young girl struggling making a decision to keep or not keep a constant reminder of that night. I will choose not to picket outside a clinic, but I will choose to show love.

Love will be responsible for what it can do.

Love.

Love won't expect our government to take care of things that God Himself has asked me to take care of.

Love will look at each one of these politicians and remember they were created by a God who knows what He is doing.

Love will remember that they have a purpose.

Perfect Love.

Dear friends, let us love one another, for love comes from God. 1 John 4:7

I had to experience God's love to learn and know it is real. Not only is love real, but that He really loves me. I liken it to many of life's experiences. Some toddlers only learn the stove is hot by feeling it for themselves. You find out if you are a roller coaster lover or hater by taking a wild and crazy ride on one. How can someone know that snow is cold and wet just by telling them? They need to experience it. How can someone know that a cannoli from Rosauer's bakery is amazing, unless they taste and experience it for themselves? I believe that others will experience love when we share love. Love. A love that changed me. A love that is so amazing- it- love wrote this book- and I am confident enough to say that this love is something you want to know about.

Whoever does not love does not know God, because God is love. 1 John 4:8

What the world needs now is love, sweet love
It's the only thing that there's just too little of
What the world needs now is love, sweet love,
No not just for some but for everyone.[2]

I come here today to type and share my heart. Which is full. Full of emotion. Full of questions. Full of concerns. Full of life. Full of 'stuff' that always needs her Jesus to wrap around it and present it to you. So please know that this presentation is just that. My heart, which I am praying He presents to you. Because in all my humanness I will mess it up. I will not type the sentence with the proper structure (My apologies to my Editor and The Engineer), I will not use all the right and fancy words (sorry to my writer friends), and I might not make sense.

We all start in Egypt. We are all born slaves. We get used to Egypt. We are comfortable with its smells and sounds. May I dare to say we like what we found, well maybe not like but we know what to expect. The routine, the pattern, the consistency, the lack of change. Egypt is different, just as different as our DNA and very personal to each one of us. Yes there are chains and bondage. But my chains have a little bit different 'clink' sound to them. Not better, prettier, easier, nope chains in Egypt are just that, chains.

Chains that clink the sounds of,
- Fear.
- Mistrust.

- Pride.
- Selfishness.
- Guilt.
- Addiction.
- Religion.

We were made to live free. We were created to live without the chains. And yet something keeps us in Egypt.

- Afraid of the wilderness.
- Too tired to walk the journey.
- Embarrassed of standing out.
- Worried we won't know which way to go.
- Comfortable with the smell, taste and view of our *little* lot in Egypt.

Making the decision to allow Him to deliver you is big; it's huge. Allowing Him to remove the chains, grab your hand and lead you out of Egypt is huge.

So where do you find yourself right now?

Are you still in Egypt?

Are you allowing the culture of false beliefs and lies to keep you in chains? Do you have a white-knuckle grip on your life plan? Are you depending on a person, place or thing? Are you bound in debt or a career?

Do you believe that He is standing there right now ready to free you? Free you so that you can walk with Him. Walk purposefully towards the Promised Land. A land you were created to live in. A land that will look nothing like Egypt, on purpose.

I want you to know you are loved by a God who thinks you are the greatest thing He ever did!

The Lord your God is in your midst,
A victorious warrior.

DO YOU KNOW I LOVE YOU?

He will exult over you with joy,
He will be quiet in His love,
He will rejoice over you with shouts of joy. Zephaniah
3:17 (New American Standard Bible)

So today is the day I have to share. Literally. I send all three-quarters of Team Hamblin back into their worlds of influence.

The Engineer with coffee mug in hand and laptop bag slung over his shoulder is off to make this world a better place. And truly he does, his laughter and sense of humor mixed with all the right calculations of airflow, pressure, weights and square footage, and he thinks I don't pay attention! Really I know this stuff, it just doesn't tickle my fancy as much as it does his, so I let him do it!

I also have to share the two shorter members of Team Hamblin today. Their sphere of influence, their school. Where today some amazing teachers will greet them, learn until their brains need a break, run out some energy, and share some laughs with their friends.

'Their sphere of influence'. What does that mean?

It's their places where they take Jesus to. Take love and spread it all around. I would be silly to sit here and think that the world won't influence them in both good and bad ways.

However, today as I clean a home that has been well loved and lived in for days, I will be praying for each one of them, praying that Jesus will be their strength, their courage, and that He keeps their chins up! For they have some important tasks to do today, they have Jesus to share in their spheres of influence.

So as hard as it for me to share I will do it knowing my three boys have a mission today.

And that's what teams do you know... they work together.

Go Team Hamblin!

Do everything in love. 1 Corinthians 16:14

Am I Running on Purpose? Am I living a life that says I follow a bunch of rules/guidelines and fill my Sunday morning schedule? Am I known for being against things and people? Lord, help me to think on this. How I truly am living? I desire to know I am loved and live like it. I pray for the awareness of the process it took for me to get here and know that The Creator has designed that same process for each one of His created. I want others to see Him, hear His voice, the voice that has called them to an abundant life.

My Prayer: Lord I pray hard right now, a passion burning inside me, that would more than anything want others to find You, fall in love with You and decide to run after You with everything they've got. Lord that the world would grow dim to us all. That we would know deep in our hearts a love that is like nothing we could ever understand, a love that truly gives us each breath, and a love that carries us to each moment. That grace and love will take us through. Not rules, not religion, not a church, not a pastor. Thank You Jesus for being the mediator, for standing in my place, to make this moment with You all possible. I love You, Amen.

A Love Without End

And he said, "Let me tell you a secret about a father's love,
A secret that my daddy said was just between us."
He said, "Daddies don't just love their children every now and then.
It's a love without end, amen, it's a love without end, amen."[1]

I'm unloading the dishwasher, refilling my tea cup, folding the load of whites and placing them back in the drawers of the soon to be wearers. As I enter the oldest boy's room I notice the blankets on the bed could be straightened. There was a time when I believed this was not 'holy work' let alone a divine moment. How could it be? I pull up the deep navy blue comforter I realize 'holy and divine moments' have been missed by me for years, and I make a vow to my Maker. To be more aware. To know that there are more amazing moments in which to partake. Really it's not about leaving and coming into them. Rather residing in them constantly.

For I am remembering early on how I had developed a regimen of writing. One in which would only take place if I had set aside the time and place. It is now that I am aware of the 'writing' that was going on even when I was not sitting at my laptop. Again it's not about getting all the words out, but rather acknowledging they went in. Into my mind, but most importantly to my heart. Not to fret if I caught them all, made sense of them all, but to gracefully admit they are there, for my faith is not in myself, but Him. His presence and promise. He fulfills. Love. Is exposure to something that gets us used to it? Makes us numb? Unaware? I have to question the possibility of becoming unaware as I am in the beginning of my journey of becoming more aware. Is that a fear? Becoming unaware, isn't that where I resided for years though? What I have been freed from? A fear of going back. How can I prevent that? And the answer bounces loudly off the brown walls that surround me, "You be aware." Prevention is in the 'be'. Being aware. Being in relationship. Be in Him. Love led me to this place today. A place of pure joy. Knowing that these are not my words that leave my fingers and enter this laptop. They are His. Love.

I am so thankful for the process. I am thankful for moments I wasn't thankful for at the time when they occurred. I am thankful for those who prayed me through. I am thankful for those who stood so close, even when I pushed. I am more aware today of moments in which He was investing. Times, peoples, seasons in which love was investing. For a day in which I would become aware. Love invested. Love that would wait. There is freedom in remembering the past. A past in which you will take and learn and grow from. Not to curse, but rather to build and strengthen. To acknowledge that the Creator can take that which seems completely tarnished, broken and lost, no good, and make holy. He can make it holy. Love knows. Love has perfect timing. Being aware right here right now that He is here, here with me. Being. I am with Him knowing that I am loved. My God. That is Love.

The enemy will come to spit fire. May my reaction be to grab tighter to His hand. I am choosing to believe, He knows. He is in control. God with me. May I trust in Him. God alone. May I be wise enough to expect the enemy's flames, and wise enough to know I need God to fight in my weakness. May my focus remain in staying in Him. Remain in Love. To a place that brings such comfort and joy, peace and contentment. For I am learning the safety of love. To trust God and not my fears and doubts. My emotions are temporary, God and His love for me is eternal.

I really am a simple girl. As you now know from reading my very 'simple' words in this book. I am easily lost in big fancy words. One Sunday the pastor was talking about 'abiding' in God. When I heard the word 'abiding' I was instantly distracted. I don't use this word in my everyday conversations. I was caught up trying to figure out what this word meant. What does it mean to abide? Am I abiding? What does abiding look like? Abide is a verb which means 'to remain'. To abide in Him. To remain in Him. To live each breath of each day with Him. Aware. In relationship. Not just checking in, but communicating with Him. A daily grounding. To seek balance. Much easier when I am remaining in Him. As I remain in Him I find no lack, no unmet need, no ache, no distraction. For there is peace, contentment, joy, fulfillment. I am fully loved.

But you, dear friends, build yourselves up in your most holy faith and pray in the Holy Spirit. **Keep yourselves in God's love** *as you wait for the mercy of our Lord Jesus Christ to bring you to eternal life. Jude 20-21 (emphasis mine)*

Remain in Him.

"As the Father has loved me, so have I loved you. Now **remain in my love**. *John 15:9 (emphasis mine)*

There are the moments that still pop up where I wonder, doubt and question. And maybe this will happen until I am free of the sin and limits of this world. Maybe they are there to serve as my desperate need to remain. Remain in Him.

Remain in love. To remain in love is God's original design for my life. And by His power I can remain here. Time spent in His love. For there is purpose behind the instruction to remain in God's love. Remaining in love heals, repairs, renews, transforms, and teaches. Remaining in love brings us closer to God. His bigness. A bigness that helps block out the world. For when I am close to God things of this world don't seem so overwhelming, scary and not fun. I have a track record for trying to scoot away, thinking I can be in control and handle things on my own. When I scoot away I find myself not content, sad, depressed, doubting and worrying and fear seems to be all around. God's arm reaches out and pulls me back in and His voice so calmly says, "Remain here daughter. I love you."

I desire to be aware. To take notice. To remain in His love. To live knowing I am loved. And to love. To be aware and still. To remain. Calm, peaceful, balanced. Seeking the continuance of this state of being. Knowing that true joy radiates in this life. Heaven on earth. To live a life of recognition of God's presence, provision and protection   All in. Submitted to my Creator. All of me. Even the parts that I am unconsciously still holding on to. Pure praise. Because of the joy in the praise. True thanks. Because of the contentment found in giving thanks. Heart abandoned to living fully in each moment for Him. Help these not to remain words typed into a journal on my laptop. Help them to be in me. In my mind, heart and soul. To stay with me. To go with me. Help me to live them today.

Remaining in Him. All along He has asked me to remain in His great amazing most awesome love for me.

My Prayer: I would love to hang here for hours and record the memories and moments that over filled the minutes, hours, days and months of this past year. The hardest thing, the best thing, something we learned and a funny memory. It was within the moments of doing life with Team Hamblin that I fell in love again, deeper, love to a depth unknown as of yet. I love being part of this Team. I love being the wife and the momma. Not because it's easy and always perfect, rather because it's not. Because then it is reliance on You, the one who fulfills me, who shows Yourself to me. To live within the realm of needing You. Needing Love. A Love without end. I desire to remain there. Amen.

Finish Strong

The Engineer always speaks words of wisdom, but I don't always recognize them as words of wisdom in the moment. I was sitting in the passenger side of our Jeep and we were talking about the excitement and energy that surrounds the start of a project. How it's much easier to be excited in the beginning of something, but that intent, passion and energy can die out. That it takes strong focus, determination and perseverance to finish something that you start.

Team Hamblin has a few mantras we like to use. One of them is, 'Finish Strong'. We have used it on the soccer field, while learning something new and when cheering each other on.

Love does that. It comes around supports us and cheers us on.

Love brings us to things and through things.

Love fills.

Love filled that deep void within me. It continues to fill.

I could sit here and tell you that love is what will fit in your spot too. But I know that me telling you might not work. For me it was a journey and a process. It took time. In all honesty it is still being worked out. I wonder if that is part of the ultimate plan. A relationship in which love keeps us close, asks us to remain, to live in balance at peace and content.

Finish Strong!

We want each of you to show this same diligence to the very end, in order to make your hope sure. Hebrews 6:11

To the very end.

I remember chanting 'finish strong' as I ran my last leg of Hood to Coast! We used this motto with the boys and their baseball game last night. I am praying this motto over the book today. I am to finish strong! Finish what God asked me to do.

I was so afraid to begin because I didn't know I could finish. When really beginning and ending weren't the purpose. The purpose was the journey, the process. The relationship.

Let perseverance finish its work so that you may be mature and complete, not lacking anything. James 1:4

Finish strong.

There's an end and final page to the book. But not to this incredible journey of knowing I'm loved. Because I'm human I will need to hear it again and again. And because He is God He will keep telling me over and over.

My Prayer: Your love is perfect and it doesn't sway, shift or falter. And most importantly Your love is not dependent on who I am. For many years I had judged Your love according to what I thought it was, how I thought it worked and I had it all wrong. I thank You Lord for a love that was so amazing that and patient. Patient to journey with me. To a point in which I am realizing how this love has been following me all along, waiting, waiting for me to become aware of its presence. A love that is always with me. A love that knows what's coming. A love that because of the nature of it fills to overflowing and then just comes out. A love that cheers me on to 'Finish Strong,' Amen.

Well Done

Agirl who was created and born in the image of God. A God who created her on purpose. A purpose that would take her many, many years to realize. There was 'stuff' all around that kept her distracted - fear, control issues, pride, stubbornness, perfectionism, running. This girl more than anything craved love. Wanted love. Needed love. Love. Pure love. Unconditional love. And yet everything she turned to wasn't what she wanted. What she tried putting in that hole was not meant to go there. People, career, shoes, food, leadership roles. None of it seemed to fill the hole. For it led to disappointment. Unmet expectations. A void. Was she not worthy of the love she was created for? She truly didn't deserve it. And she wasn't quite sure that grace was even for her.

For many years it seemed so much easier to keep running and doing. In doing that, there was never time to heal. Truly heal. Running kept things covered. Things she didn't want others to see. And truth be known she didn't want to see it either.

Running. For she knew how to do that, and the hurt is buffered. The pain was not as noticeable. God was in His God role. There was no relationship and intimacy. She wasn't worthy. She would have to try harder or just come to an acceptance that this was as good as it could be for her, but that's when God broke her. For love doesn't let us settle. Love doesn't make us work harder. Not love. Not the love we were created out of and for. This love captures us, causes us to sit, allows us to heal, and is patient enough to stay with us. This love mellows us long enough. Long enough to heal; truly heal. In this healing she starts to see who she is. Who she truly is! She sees that she had an unhealthy perspective. For she created a God. One who wasn't true, pure, holy and righteous. She had put words in His mouth. Out of her brokenness, out of her 'owies', from behind a wall of hiding, she made Him up. And in her healing she realized He isn't man made, He can't be controlled, or dictated, and that He knew this all along about her… and that is how she is coming to see that love, pure love is beyond all things. She hears Him. She asks Him to keep speaking. She desires to listen. But **more** than listen she desires for this love to overtake her. To engulf her. To change her. For this love will change broken unhealthy thoughts. This love will heal the soul. This love will allow a close relationship with her Creator. This love will be right.

Love that comes to us, wraps its arms around us. Right where we are. Right in the middle of our confused, busy, chaotic, unknown, dirty mess. Love wraps His arms around us. And keeps repeating over and over, "I love you." Love waits with us. Love confirms over and over it's not going anywhere. Love cannot be chased away. For love is ultimately in control. Love doesn't move or change, rather we move away. We are not comfortable with the purity and holiness of love. Because of sin. Sin makes us feel we are not good enough, not ready, not deserving. Sin clouds our vision. Sin blocks our ears. Sin scares our hearts and souls. Not allowing love to penetrate. Sin helps us to create our version of what God is. Sin leads us to falsely believe we are in control and thus we call the shots for love. We get so tightly lost and wrapped up in the lies, disgust and we end up buried. **But** we are not beyond the reach of love. Love never stops seeing us. Love is there, always has been and always will be. Love doesn't leave His children. Love doesn't give up. Love can't. It's not in the character of love. Love continues its mantra, "I love you." Patiently waiting until we hear the words. Hear them, and then love guides them into our hearts. For our hearts need to know. Need to know that these are not just words.

Love guides itself into our hearts where our true created self-awakes to **knowing** this is it. The 'It' we were created for. The purposeful relationship with our Creator. One in which we can't truly put into words, but one that must be personally and intimately experienced by each one of us with our Creator. There isn't a right or wrong way to experience love, but rather the way. The way in which our amazing Creator designed it to be. Every detail He worked out. Every detail. The places He needs to take you, the people He brings into your life. For with love comes healing, comfort, peace, contentment, joy, transformation. Love knows the process. For when we let love lead then we are where we should be. And through the whole relationship love will continue to whisper and sometimes shout "I love you." Love knows right when we need to hear it. Love knows the volume at which we need to hear it.

Love has perfect timing. Love also knows when we need to experience it. Intimate and personal to each one of us. When we start to allow love to replace the darkness of sin and self we start to see all that love is and does around us. We hear a child's laugh or see an elderly man smile and realize love is so close. We feel the warm embrace of a friend we haven't seen in years and realize love is there and gifting us this moment. When we are not clouded with sin, love seems more. Perfect love also respects free will. Which is something we come to accept during the relationship. Many questions are asked about free will. Why's abound? Choices and decisions that could have saved much time and heartache if not allowed to be made. But again, love knows the perfect process.

Love's ultimate goal is to have all of us. All our mind, heart and soul. Every ounce of us. Our fears, doubts, questions, worries, and most importantly our sin. For love already took it all, on a cross. So why do we hold onto it and carry it? He shouts enough already, "Stop, let me love you." Purification, holiness, righteousness, or more simply put, 'cleaning up our mess' cannot be done by us. It has never been done by a human and never will. Only love can clean us up. Only by allowing love to overtake our minds, hearts and souls do we experience the relationship we were created for. Sometimes our mess is so comfortable we don't see it as a mess. It's not until love starts to get our attention that we see the mess for what it is, a mess.

Whether it is legalism, church girl, pride, perfectionism, the need for control, or people pleasing, a mess is a mess! Love shines light on the darkness we seem to think we were meant to live in. Love doesn't just point it out, but in the true and perfect nature of love it shows us we were created for more, for better, for true purpose. A relationship in which when we allow love to be, our mess becomes less. And when our mess becomes less we become more of what we were designed to be. Living lives filled with love. Love totally for ourselves and love to share. One cannot truly love how our Creator intended us to love until we ourselves know we are loved. This book is from life lived with my Jesus. Learning to be loved. Walking in the day-to-day life holding tight to His hand. Learning to listen, learning to trust. Learning to be loved. This book holds more than words. It holds years, moments, lessons, truths, time, tears, heart break, loss, gifts, disappointments, and blessings. Most importantly this book is the journey of my God asking my heart a question;

"Nichole, do you know I love you?"

And me responding with my whole mind, heart and soul, **"I DO!"**

I keep asking that the God of our Lord Jesus Christ, the glorious Father, may give you the Spirit of wisdom and revelation, so that you may know Him better. I pray also that the eyes of your heart may be enlightened in order that you may know the hope to which He has called you, the riches of His glorious inheritance in the saints, and His incomparably great power for us who believe. Ephesians 1:17-19

May the grace of the Lord Jesus Christ, and the love of God, and the fellowship of the Holy Spirit be with you all. 2 Corinthians 13:14

I'm gonna run this race
To hear You say well done.[1]

My Prayer: Lord we want to see You… to hear Your voice, the voice that has called us to abundant life. Your love. We don't deserve it, can't earn it, and will never truly wrap our heads around the why You give it, but Father God, thank You. May we know today in this very moment God that You think of us loves us immensely. May we **Sit** with You each day, so we are able to **Stand** in Your strength, equipped to **Walk** or **Run** through each moment in Love. Amen.

Endnotes

Epigraph

1. "Toni Morrison Quotes," Goodreads, accessed September 21, 2011, https://www.goodreads.com/quotes/321-if-there-s-a-book-that-you-want-to-read-but

What the Professionals Might Call the Prologue

1. Meyer, Joyce. Eat the Cookie-- Buy the Shoes: Giving Yourself Permission to Lighten Up. FaithWords, 2010.

Sit Down

1. Lucado, Max. The 3:16 Promise, Thomas Nelson, 2007, p. 143.

Fighting the Sit

1. Shirer, Priscilla Evans. One in a Million: Journey to Your Promised Land. B & H, 2010.

2. Ibid., 42

Sitting on the Porch

1. "Mark Twain Quotes," Goodreads, accessed , https://www.goodreads.com/quotes/38762-writing-is-easy-all-you-have-to-do-is-cross

Learn to Be Still

1. Eagles. "Learn To Be Still." Eagles Hell Freezes Over, 1994.

Being vs. Doing

1. "being". The American Heritage® Dictionary of Idioms by Christine Ammer. Houghton Mifflin Company. 12 Feb. 2018. <Dictionary.com http://www.dictionary.com/browse/being>.

2. Francessa Battistelli, "Holy Sprit." If We're Honest, 2014.

Let It All Go

1. "William Wordsworth Quotes," Brainy Quote, accessed July 24th 2017, https://www.brainyquote.com/quotes/william_wordsworth_108633

The Void

1. Meyer, Joyce. Eat the Cookie-- Buy the Shoes: Giving Yourself Permission to Lighten Up. FaithWords, 2010, p. 161.

2. Amazing Grace. Dir. Michael Apted. Perf. Ioan Gruffudd and Albert Finney. Walden Media, 2007. Netflix. Web, 1-21-13.

Can You Hear Me Now?

1. Haseltine, Dan. "Love Song for a Savior." Jars of Clay. 1994.

How Will I Know?

1. George Merrill and Shannon Rubicam. "How will I know?", Whitney Houston, 1985.

Now Stand

1. R.E.M. "Stand." Green, 1988.

The Way That I am

1. JJ Heller. "What Love Really Means.", When I'm With You, 2010.

Realization of Who I Created God to Be

1. Mercy Me. "Word of God.", Spoken For, 2002.

The Heart of the Matter

1. Don Henley. "The Heart of the Matter.", End of the Innocence. 1989.

2. "freedom". Dictionary.com Unabridged. Random House, Inc. 13 Feb. 2018. <Dictionary.com http://www.dictionary.com/browse/freedom>.

You are God Alone

1. Mark Altrogge. "I Stand in Awe of You", Sovereign Grace Praise. 1987.

2. Tozer, A.W., The Pursuit of God. Christian Publications, INC. Harrisburg, PA. March 24, 2011. Kindle Edition.

What Love Is This?

1. Mick Jones. "I Want to Know What Love Is?", Foreigner. Agent Provocateur. 1984.

2. Lincoln Brewster, Mia Fieldes, Kari Jobe. "What Love is This?", Where I Find You. 2012.

3. Brandon Heath, "I'm Not Who I Was.", Don't Get Comfortable. 2007.

Enough

1. Hillsong Worship, "Cornerstone.", Hillsong Music. 2012.

2. Jason Castro, "Enough.", Only on a Mountain. 2013.

Stand by Me

1. Ben E. King, Jerry Leiber and Mike Stoller, "Stand By Me.", Don't Play That Song. Ben E. King. 1961.

I Do

1. Chris Tomlin and Louie Giglio. "Enough", Not To Us. Chris Tomlin. 2002.

2. Chris McClarney. "Your Love Never Fails." Your Love Never Fails. Jesus Culture. 2008.

3. Burpo, Todd, and Lynn Vincent. Heaven Is for Real: a Little Boy's Astounding Story of His Trip to Heaven and Back. W Publishing Group, 2014.

Focus/Balance/Transition

1. "Frank Kafka Quotes," Goodreads, accessed July 24, 2017, https://www.goodreads.com/quotes/13148-writing-is-utter-solitude-the-descent-into-the-cold-abyss

2. Russell K Carter. "Standing on the Promises", 1886, accessed February 14,2018, http://library.timelesstruths.org/music/Standing_on_the_Promises/.

3. Chris Eaton and Margaret Becker. "No Greater Love.",Kalediscope. Rachel Lampa, 2002.

Walk This Way

1. Chris Eaton and Margaret Becker. "No Greater Love.",Kalediscope. Rachel Lampa, 2002.

More Than Words

1. Tozer, A.W., The Pursuit of God. Christian Publications, INC. Harrisburg, PA. March 24, 2011. Kindle Edition.

2. Gary Cherone and Nuno Bettencourt., "More Than Words", Extreme II, Extreme, 1990.

3. Jason Gray and Jason Ingram., "More Like Falling in Love.", Everything Sad Is Coming Untrue, Jason Gray, 2009.

4. Meyer, Joyce. Eat the Cookie-- Buy the Shoes: Giving Yourself Permission to Lighten Up. FaithWords, 2010, p. 40.

Love's Been Following You

1. Twila Paris. "Loves Been Following You.", Where I Stand, 1996.

2. Brian Johnson, Christa Black Gifford, and Jeremy Riddle. "One Thing Remains.", Come Away, Jesus Culture. 2010.

ENDNOTES

Obedience

1. John H. Sammis., "Trust and Obey.", 1887, accessed February 14, 2018, http://library.timelesstruths.org/music/Trust_and_Obey/.

Walking on Sunshine

1. "Walt Whitman Quotes." BrainyQuote.com. Xplore Inc, 2018. 14 February 2018. https://www.brainyquote.com/quotes/walt_whitman_384665.

My Own Walk - Others Have Theirs

1. Sheehan, George. 4 November 2012, Runners World Facebook Page.

One Thing Remains

1. Hybels, Bill. The Power of a Whisper. Hearing God. Having the guts to respond. Zondervan. 2010.

Self-Control

1. Jennifer Kennedy Dean., Set Apart: A 6-Week Study of the Beatitudes. New Hope Publishers. 2009. P. 166.

Transition to Run

1. Toby McKeehan, Aaron Rice, Jamie Moore, and Cary Barlowe., "Made to Love." Portable Sounds. TobyMac. 2007.

2. Meyer, Joyce. Eat the Cookie-- Buy the Shoes: Giving Yourself Permission to Lighten Up. FaithWords, 2010, p. 138.

Because You Love Me

1. Meledandri, Chris, et al. Despicable Me. Universal, 2010.

2. Diane Warren. "Because You Love Me.", Falling Into You., Celine Dion. 1996.

Marathon/Endurance/Pacer

1. Henry Ford., "Running Quotes for the Runner.", All About Marathon Training. Accessed November 2014. https://www.all-about-marathon-training.com/runningquotes.html.

2. "endure". Online Etymology Dictionary. Douglas Harper, Historian. 14 Feb. 2018. <Dictionary.com http://www.dictionary.com/browse/endure>.

Run-Rest-Repeat

1. Yoga Is: A Transformational Journey. Written and directed by Suzanne Bryant. Performances by Micahel Franti, Russell Simmons, Christy Turlington., Magnolia Home Entertainment. 2012. Accessed 2013 on Netflix.

2. "Be Still My Soul- In You I Rest.", Jesus, Firm Foundation: Hymns Of Worship. Kari Jobe.

Running on Purpose

1. "Mother Teresa Quotes." BrainyQuote.com. Xplore Inc, 2018. 14 February 2018. https://www.brainyquote.com/quotes/mother_teresa_108724

2. Hal David and Burt Bacharach. "What The World Needs Now-Is Love Sweet Love.", This is Jackie DeShannon. Jackie DeShannon. Imperial Records. 1965.

A Love Without End

1. Aaron Barker., "A Love Without End.", Livin' It Up., George Strait., MCA. 1990.

Well Done

1. Chad Cates, Moriah Peters and Jason Walker., "Well Done.", I Choose Jesus. Moriah Peters., Reunion. 2012.

About the Author

Nichole Hamblin is wife to The Engineer, momma to two boys, a blogger, and speaker. An American child of the 70s, her faithful readers like her relatable, conversational and honest writing style. She is a work-in-progress who is passionate about shoes, good food, Chai tea, her family, running, reading, and taking naps. She has learned that Jesus' love is everything. As a recovering 'perfectionist control addict' she is consumed with learning to lead others on the pursuit of love.

Nichole can be found enjoying her team around their dining table, where stories from the day, laughter, encouragement and life lessons are shared often. Her goals are to keep her growing boys fed, spread love and continue to explore the beautiful islands of New Zealand where Team Hamblin is currently residing.

You can connect with Nichole on social media www.facebook.com/nicholehamblinofficial/, Instagram nicholehamblin_writer or on her website: www.nicholehamblin.com.